# DRIVEN
# BY STEAM

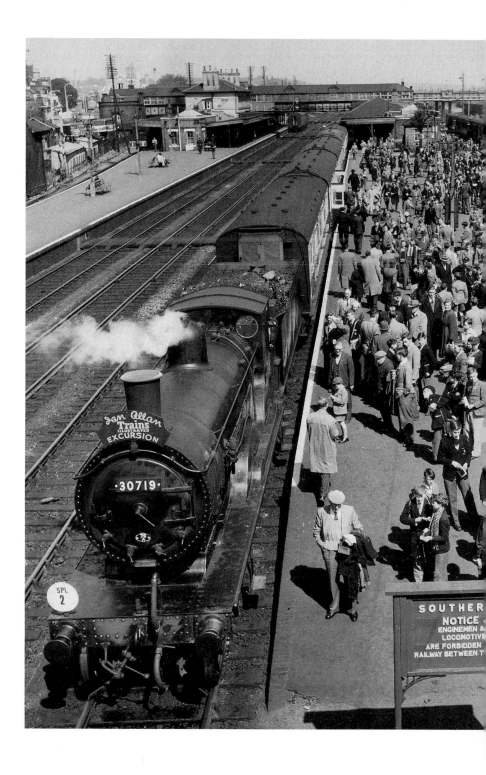

# DRIVEN
# BY STEAM

*Ian Allan*

*Publishing*

First published 1992

ISBN 0 7110 2118 X

© Ian Allan Ltd 1992

Published by Ian Allan Ltd,
Shepperton, Surrey; and printed by
Ian Allan Printing Ltd at their works
at Coombelands in Runnymede,
England.

*Previous page:*
**An early 1950s visit to Eastleigh. Crowds pour
out on the platform prior to trekking to the
Works.**

*Below:*
**An early shop window display. One of Terry
Holder's first innovations.**

# Contents

# 1

# Joining the Southern Railway

It was probably my parents' fault because they employed a nursemaid whose father was a signalman at Horsham in what was then deepest Sussex, for in those very early days I was often taken into the box to watch the trains go by and see the silvery levers pulled. So I grew up with one desire, to be stationmaster at Waterloo which seemed to be the zenith of any railwayman's career objective and my father even gave me an old top hat to prepare myself. I then discovered that actually the general manager was even more important so I switched my target to his seat.

I was born at Christ's Hospital School just outside Horsham where my father was Steward, a kind of amalgam of Bursar and Estate Manager and a post which exists today as does the house 'Cornerways' in which I made my advent on an expectant world. My parents were both the eldest of fairly large families so I had masses of cousins, uncles and aunts which was all very jolly. Some had made good, some had gone into the Church for the Allans have a long connection with the cloth. The star turn was my mother's brother who rose to the dizzy height of being Treasury Solicitor and getting a GCB for it; during the abdication of Edward VIII he hit the headlines in his capacity as HM Procurator General. Quite a useful chap as I was later to find out, especially when on my father's death he got probate through in 24 hours flat. Another was senior partner of Knight, Frank & Rutley whilst his brother had founded and become MD of Southdown Motor Services. So I had some of the right connections and went through the usual run of middle class education, kindergarten, prep school and eventually to St Paul's, getting into which was the only examination I ever managed to pass in a totally undistinguished academic career, and yet I consider I had, in fact, a first class education.

In 1935 the family moved into a super house in Staines. Its enormous garden full of interesting paths soon became to me imaginary railway tracks with bicycles simulating trains. The second storey was made over to me for model railways and following a magnificent Christmas present of a set of purpose made trestle tables, work started on an elaborate 'O' gauge railway. Being made to go to boarding school had greatly interfered with the development of the railway so that when I was ultimately released to go to St Paul's, not only could I enjoy the benefits of home life but also actually

*Above:*
**Where it all began. 225/7 Laleham Road, Staines — a private house which,
fortunately, had two street numbers and looked impressive on the first letterheads.**

have the pleasure of commuting by train every day from Staines to Hammersmith. Educational standards were always high at St Paul's and I learnt a lot there — mostly how to thieve and cheat — for in those days these two qualities were essential for mere survival. Homework was massive and, as I was (indeed am) not much good at reading anything more than 100 words, virtually impossible. Needless to say, I never made the five passes with two credits necessary to get a School Certificate in those days, let alone Matriculation standard.

St Paul's had one or two redeeming features. The Smee Society was one. It involved visits almost every Saturday, and sometimes during the week, to establishments remotely connected with engineering, railways included. It also had an O gauge model railway in the bowels of the earth which was never finished — probably still is not — and operated on a shoe string. So fine was the string that to reduce the current from the 110V dc main, a few 100W bulbs were wired in series which seemed to produce a track voltage of around 12V dc which was fine; unless, of course, you touched one of the trains with one hand at the same time as something metallic with the other. You were then guaranteed a high amperage 110V dc shock which made you very cautious in the future. I suppose we learnt more about electrics, mooching about with that railway than ever we did in the physics lab.

It was virtually obligatory to join the OTC and as my father was a true soldier, having been a 2nd/Lt — no less — in World War 1 and my brother having risen to the unique (in the SPSOTC) rank of Quartermaster Sergeant (he was sadly killed at Singapore in 1942 as a Lieutenant RA) I was duly enrolled. I could never keep step and although my arms drill was reasonably good, I did manage the unpardonable sin of losing my rifle during a field day on Chobham Common (or it would have been a sin if I hadn't found someone else's lying around) but that was only a detail, for at a following camp, which I found just about the most dreadful experience possible to inflict on any adolescent, I managed to clout my knee with some solid object or vice versa, which having gone wrong internally cost me my left leg at the age of 15. No great shakes this and I was able to take it all in my metaphorical and physical stride; within six weeks I was walking, even riding a bike again thanks to the miracles of Messrs Dessouters of 73 Baker Street, limb makers by appointment. I went back to school to take my second swipe at School Cert and meanwhile decided that it was time to get to work.

It was not all that easy to get a railway job in early 1939. However, my father had a wide circle of friends and often found himself sitting next to the right people at dinners: he happened fortuitously to find himself one night adjacent to G. S. Szlumper, General Manager of the Southern Railway, just the right chap. Szlumper organised an appointment for me to see his No 2, J. B. (later Sir John) Elliot, who did his utmost to dissuade me from joining the Southern, advising that I was likely to do better in almost any other sphere of life; but I did not break that easily and probably to keep me quiet and get on with his own job, he offered me the post of a temporary Grade 5 Clerk in the General Manager's office at 15s (75p) a week.

I jumped at it. I was not so much interested in the wage packet; all I wanted was to get into my beloved Southern Railway and all the benefits and privileges it would bring. I started work on 16 July 1939 in the Publicity and PR Department at Waterloo and was set to work without any training whatsoever to produce excursion advertisements for local papers throughout Southern England. Apart from learning that there were such exotic papers as the *Kent Messenger*, the *Western Morning News* and the *Brighton Argus*, I had a pretty scant idea of what I was supposed to be doing and I have no doubt that a lot of local rags published a lot of rubbish as a result. But not for long, for within six weeks war had been declared and all these excursions promptly stopped — virtually for ever — for nothing like the programme of special seaside excursions happened on the same scale again.

There was a considerable hiatus for the lesser breeds like me, for we were all stagnating between the shaky peace and outright war and it gave me time to explore Waterloo from its subterranean passages via the platform lifts to the rooftop to which I discovered the doorway to an exciting new world. Two extraordinary things struck me: firstly that no-one in the Publicity Department, except the Chief Clerk, one S. K. Packham (an ex-LBSCR man who knew not only every 'Brighton' locomotive by name and number but the driver's too) had any knowledge of, or apparently interest in, railways. They obviously viewed it as something rather peculiar that I should be wanting to spend my own spare time riding on and investigating trains, locomotives, stations and other appendages of what they considered merely their meal ticket.

My appointment as a 'temporary' clerk was for a six month trial period at the end of which I was told that I could stay though I would for ever be 'temporary' as I could not pass the medical and, therefore, could not join the superannuation scheme. The good news was that my remuneration would rise to £1 per week.

As the war gathered momentum, staff began to leave and fewer of us had to mop up the thinning activities of publicity, public relations and advertising and to get involved in the railway companies' war effort from the inside. I do not know quite what we did or why we did it but I am sure we did it very well.

The motormen and guards of Waterloo got their mess room relocated next to the PR department and we shared the first floor 'facilities' with them whilst the clerical staff were similarly accorded the privilege of using 'The Dive', a rather foul converted arch which dispensed quite disgusting tea at 1d a cup and even more dreadful cheese rolls at 2½d a throw. At least lunch was cheap at 3½d but all the mates from the cab and van foregathered there as well. It was, of course, open sesame to someone as nutty as I was to get on the front or rear end of trains whenever I felt like a ride somewhere — especially if I could persuade dear old Packham to lend me the Office Pass for the weekend which was, of course, strictly against the rules. So the railway bug bit deeper and deeper.

So far as my official work was concerned, I became quite accidentally the (very) sidekick of Ben Webb, editor of the *Southern Railway Magazine* and head of the 'publications' section. He would require me to sit with him for hours on end watching him make up the magazine and other printed works from proofs and block pulls; my function was to trim the edges with his scissors and paste the bits into position. Eventually I graduated to being allowed to deal with the most dreary section of the magazine — 'Staff Changes' which were a mass of names in tiny print which I had to check, recheck and proof read. It bored me stiff but at least I was on my own at last. I realised later that all the time spent with Ben Webb was not wasted but stood me in good stead for I learnt the really hard way everything about magazine editorial and production — besides which it enabled me to go to the printers at Islington two or three times a week and incur 'expenses'. The tram fare from Westminster Bridge Road to Islington was 2d, a cup of tea was 2d and I reckoned it was fair to charge 1s a trip. But the SR did not, and my reckoning was quickly cut down to 6d a shot. Anyway, the tram ride took me through the Kingsway subway which was always exciting.

One day the news was flashed to us that the offices were to be evacuated from Waterloo to Elmstead Woods where the company had purchased a large house known as 'Sitka'. This was in line with the general policy, the GM's own office had gone to the Deepdene Hotel at Dorking (the sale of which Uncle Gordon Cannon had effected through KF&R) whilst the LMS lot had gone to 'The Grove' at Watford, hence the code names 'Grove Specials' for the important trains and 'Deepdene Specials' for not quite so VIP dittos. For all of us this was a great inconvenience: if I came from Staines it was not so bad a journey via Waterloo Junction but coming up from Christ's Hospital where my father's office (and home) had moved for the duration, was awful.

The company laid on a daily lorry with a canvas tilt from Wimbledon to East Croydon and on to 'Sitka'. This had loose forms in it so that everyone fell on the floor at the slightest change of direction but we were all young and it was part of the fun — to start with. The very unforeseeing planners of 1940 had not foreseen that the Battle of Britain would be shot out just over Elmstead Woods and many a German bomb would be scattered over the south-east approaches. During an air raid, with a liberal sprinkling of incendiary bombs and even more flak dropping from the sky from our own anti-aircraft guns, it was not terribly comforting to ride about in an unstable lorry with only a thin sheet of canvas for protection. Going by train was not much better. On one occasion I came up from Elmstead Woods, looked out of the window to see why we had stopped to see a bomb blow up the track behind us whilst one had already knocked out the way ahead. We walked to St John's station and took shelter in a greengrocer's shop only to find our onward progress by tram blocked by myriad fire hosepipes across the road. Happily on that occasion a car stopped and offered a lift, but these interrupted and hazardous journeys to and from the office were standard practice.

So as soon as the Battle of Britain was over and the Kentish skies were clear, the foresighted railway management sent us back rejoicing to Waterloo. Our glee at going home was slightly muted when V1 and V2 rockets started to hit Central London. Indeed we all wished we were back at Elmstead Woods for there were several nasty moments — like the day a 'doodlebug' landed on the bus stop in York Road causing many fatalities and at the same time bringing down every pane of glass in the station roof and

*Above:*
**A young Ian Allan sorting out a problem with an engine driver at Waterloo in 1944.**

most of the windows as well, resulting in further casualties. How the railway operators and engineers coped during these air raids was little short of miraculous, wonders were worked in speedy repairs and by and large the train services were pretty good.

My railway enthusiasm nearly landed me in deep trouble on one occasion. My grandmother lived at Burgess Hill which was within a 10 mile exclusion zone from the coast. My parents went frequently to do their filial duties and on one occasion I went with them. I wandered off to watch the trains on the Brighton main line and took a camera with me. After an hour, a real Sussex Mr Plod arrived on his bicycle and averred that I was acting in a suspicious manner and what was I doing in Burgess Hill? 'Visiting my grandmother' as a response did not go down too well and he arrested me and marched me to the Police Station where I was interviewed by a very stern and serious inspector who equally disbelieved the grandmother explanation and was convinced I was a German parachutist or at least a fifth columnist. Ultimately I was identified and released but not until the film had been confiscated for development and subsequent inspection. I heard no more. I was a rotten photographer anyway.

One of the more radical effects of German bombardment was the damage done to Durnsford Road power station which effectively reduced the third rail electricity supply to something less than three quarters of normal. This resulted in all electric trains travelling at reduced speeds for months on end, though this had the benefit of saving at least one chap's life. One night in the black-out I was at Dorking North and in the tiny light of the foreman's lamp a shunter was uncoupling two units. He was about to get back on the narrow cleaners' platform by hauling himself up on the buffers when he let out a piercing scream. We thought he was joking and told him to get up: he tried again and screamed again. Further light on the subject proved him to be standing on the conductor rail and completing the circuit every time he touched the train. Thank heaven for 450V and not 650!

# 2

# Harnessing the Southern to Work

I often wonder how I survived my days on the Southern, for Health & Safety regulations had not been invented and I was continually wandering around main lines fairly regardless of conductor rails which I am sure would have done a good job on my tin leg if contact had been made. I once walked the length of the Waterloo & City line dodging trains in the occasional refuge in the tunnel side. But I did survive.

Wartime privations and many of the more exciting hobbies and pastimes being unavailable for the 'duration' probably stimulated the ever present, though perhaps latent, interest in railways. In my own younger days a friend, Geoffrey Curtis (later to become a brigadier and PM's adviser on matters ecclesiastical) and I had spent hours cycling either to Weybridge or Iver to watch the trains go by on Saturdays. I do not think we ever actually took down engine names or numbers but certainly they were all noted. Slowly we had begun to recognise locomotive classes and different types of rolling stock which I suppose was the basis for the first books on the subject. So far as the office was concerned, I, being more or less the only chap with a smattering of knowledge of locomotives, had all the enquiries coming into the department passed to me and the routine was to send out a duplicated list of engine names and numbers. This was not a lot of help because it only prompted more detailed questions and we only provided details of named engines. As an aid to deal with all this, S. K. Packham produced for me a notebook with more or less all the Southern locos, their classes and their shed allocations which we perfected with the help of the famous John Pelham Maitland, the shedmaster at Nine Elms.

'Why do we not get this booklet printed and sell it to the punters and make a little profit for the Company?' I naively asked. The response was heavily negative so I sought an audience of the PRO himself, one Cuthbert Grasemann, a fiery individual and a considerable bully of his underlings, several of whom were known to emerge from his room with posters around their necks. Tentatively I asked for permission to publish on my own account and to my surprise got a quick and encouraging positive reply but a warning that I did it at my own risk and expense.

The idea was so simple: a numerical list of loco numbers with their class and a table at the end of the book giving all the details of each class so that one could relate the number to the name (if any) and to such details as tractive effort, diameter of driving wheels etc. There was at no time any thought that these numbers would be ticked off as seen or become a source of collecting anything; that happened later, for there was big drama on the way. Packham and I put the finishing touches to the manuscript bringing in also the redoubtable O. J. Morris for a final check. Now perhaps it should be said that all these chaps who started to get involved with this list of SR locos were regular contributors to the *Southern Railway Magazine*. As soon as the manuscript was ready I awaited the daily visit to the office from McCorquodales' rep — for 'McCorks' and Waterlows did virtually all the SR's printing work from special traffic notices to glossy brochures. That morning the usual rep was sick and his sidekick Willie Brett was doing the honours. I buttonholed him and asked him to quote me for 2,000 copies of a 6in x 4in 16-page book. He looked at the manuscript somewhat askance but went off with it and soon 'phoned to say they could do it for £42 but how was I going to pay? I made reassuring noises and he decided to take the chance. The 6in x 4in size was chosen as right for the pocket and 2000 x 1s would cover the costs plus a bit.

Speculation of 5s 6d for a small classified advert in *Railway World* followed and surprise, surprise the bob postal orders started to roll in. Almost 2,000 of them had arrived and once I had paid the printing bill less postage, stationery and other overheads I was left with a quite unexpected and unlooked for profit. Then the thunderbolt struck. O. V. S. Bulleid, the Southern's Chief Mechanical Engineer, got wind of the book, stormed into Grasemann and demanded its suppression — presumably on the grounds that he had not been consulted and how dare a mere PRO give permission for something to be published about *his* engines without his knowledge or consent.

The poor author/publisher then landed on the mat to be attacked by Grasemann and ordered not to publish the book on pain of 'not only the sack but legal action too'. Protestations that authorisation to proceed had been received fell on very stony ground and deaf ears — 'Get out' was his final riposte. Stuck between 2,000 paid up customers and a chopper from the boss concentrated thought remarkably: should I (a) submit and lose all my investment; (b) publish and be damned; (c) send a copy to the Chairman quickly and (d) see what happens. I decided on courses (b) and (c); the Chairman, Robert Holland Martin, got his copy and a note from the author within five minutes and, amazingly, next morning a highly commendatory letter arrived from him welcoming the book as a useful source of information and congratulating the author on his enterprise in producing it. Messrs Bulleid and Grasemann's ace thus nicely trumped, the situation changed remarkably and not only was the publication not damned but co-operation for the future extended. However, further authorial sorties into the CME's drawing office where friendly assistance had come from Bernard Anwell, another devoted Southern loco enthusiast and others, were banned.

Came thoughts for the need of a quick reprint. McCorks were happy: they had their £42 under their belt and were ready for more. O. J. Morris further titivated the presentation and suggested the title *abc of Southern Locomotives* as it sounded more interesting than the original *Southern Locomotives* and anyway the classes were listed in abc order. He did not like 'I. Allan' and proposed the complete name.

Thus 'abc' and 'Ian Allan' were really the brain child of O. J. Morris who himself was an extraordinary character and quite a nutter in his own peculiar and lovable way. Grossly overweight and generally pretty unhealthy, he lived in an utter mess at 304 Beulah Hill, West Norwood. His house was cluttered with railwayana from LBSCR signals to models and myriad books and magazines which were never cleaned from one year to the next. His model railway was unbelievable. If he came to a door, a cupboard or a stair, he simply cut through it to run the permanent way through. All his door furniture had been replaced with LBSCR carriage door handles. Needless to say, he was a bachelor. He always smelt of TCP, drank tea all day long out of a two-pint 'jorum' into which he put his sugar ration, using it up on the first day; he then resorted to golden syrup as a tea sweetener and towards the end of the ration period had to use expensive though unrationed honey. He was a marvellous photographer and writer, though ponderous in the extreme, and it was a very frustrating business to get anything out of him punctually. But he contributed greatly to the early life of Ian Allan books and we all liked him a lot.

It was natural after the first success with the Southern that the other railways should be tackled, so I had a go at the GWR — with disastrous results. The first attempt was riddled with errors but the reviews were jolly good and I was soon put right and Bernard Anwell came to the rescue and virtually put the second (and accurate) edition together. The GWR was a very withdrawn company and made no noise at all about the book, they studied studiously to ignore it, steadfastly refusing even to reply to letters.

Then I was sent for by 'Mr MacLeod' to go to Waterloo's Room 20. A. B. MacLeod was a senior officer and another *Southern Railway Magazine* contributor and, I was to discover, a dedicated nut when it came to railways. 'Do the LMS' he ordered in his whimsically humorous way but I was hesitant as I knew nothing about the LMS; it was some organisation that operated north of Watford and all I had really seen of it was Oerlikon electric trains at Earl's Court and Richmond and trains coming into Euston which were invariably late. Mindful of the trouble with Mr Bulleid, I was cautious but Mac said he would prepare the text if I could get the blessing and the pictures. Parents came in useful again, they were on friendly terms with the local butcher, George Reeves, in Staines; aforesaid butcher was the royal warrant holder to supply meat to Windsor Castle. Lord Wigram was the grand panjandrum who oversaw the meat in the royal apartments or something but more importantly, he was a director of the LMS. So bingo, out came all the pictures, dimensions and details of the LMS fleet. All were fed up to Room 20 and the first LMS book appeared on some extraordinary cream-coloured prewar art paper which McCorks had managed to dredge up from their cellars. Generously the real author agreed to our joint names appearing on the cover though he had really done all the work for which he expected no recompense, other than the brief acknowledgement of his contribution.

Ditto the LNER. Again father knew the right chap in the shape of Lord Leathers, Minister of Transport, who fired off a shot to the General Manager which eventually produced an obviously reluctant response from George Dow, the PRO. But enough ultimately came forth to get this railway dealt with and the set was complete. The haughty and imperious George Dow eventually descended from his perch and became a real friend though as an author he was the most pernickety and irascible chap you could possibly deal with. But then he was a purist and demanded accuracy and quality and rightly so, too. He and I produced one of the most detailed histories of any railway ever written, referred to by one reviewer as 'Dow's majestic trilogy', *Great Central* in three volumes.

The family, who were all working during the day, frantically dealt with the flood of mail orders that came pouring in. None of us ever got to bed before midnight and finally it got the better of us: we just could not cope. Help had to be sought so we sold stocks of the four titles to various people and just doled out the unopened letters for them to deal with as satellite mail order houses. Our assistants included chaps in the office at Waterloo, the neighbours at Staines and eventually even the station staff at Christ's Hospital station.

I was very attached to Christ's Hospital station and in my leisure hours spent a lot of time at this magnificent station with its seven platforms, three signalboxes, six passengers (apart from the School 'specials' at the beginning and end of terms) and a dozen or so staff. I learned my first lesson in life there when the Stationmaster touched me for a fiver which he never repaid, though we were all rewarded when 'my' staff at the station caught him out with his fingers in the till and he was reduced to the ranks and transferred to the goods department at Brighton. Since then I have heeded Polonius' advice:

> *'Neither a borrower nor a lender be'.*

In the office at Waterloo, two chaps, Herbert Oakley and George Drury, were both able to supplement their income by this simple home work effort. Willie Brett was already doing a bomb from 33 Knollys Road, Streatham, the pronunciation of which caused many a problem; meanwhile, at the extraordinary venue of Christ's Hospital station, a great selling operation was set up in the booking office. The station was normally run by a stationmaster who had other responsibilities but actually operated by a couple of porter–signalmen and a female porter (at that time very unusual). Mr Wally Smith, Mr Vic Eaton and Miss French (a very up-market porter in a very ill-fitting uniform) called themselves the SEF Agency and really went to town. They actually managed to attract customers to come to Christ's Hospital station to purchase our wares and thus a bit of business was generated for the Southern Railway Co. So effective were these agencies that not only did they take on board the mail I was receiving but actually started creating their own businesses. And none of them was ever a bad debt.

I have already mentioned my personal connection with Christ's Hospital School and although I did not derive my education in the place, I was very closely associated with it. So perhaps it was not surprising that the profits from the first books should have been pointed in the direction of that charity and in 1944, at the tender age of 22, I was appointed a governor of the Foundation and have maintained close links ever since.

Although most of the sales were coming by way of postal orders there was a stirring amongst the shops and the first trade orders came from W. H. Smith & Son for 12 copies and then a blockbuster from A. W. Hambling of Cecil Court, Charing Cross Road for 100 *abc Southern Locomotives* (which actual document is carefully framed and displayed in the Group offices at Shepperton), Cotterell & Co of Birmingham and Norman Kerr of Grange-over-Sands were runners up. Trade orders, of course, opened up a whole new field of credit trading and discounts, something not previously encountered, and there was some amazement that $33\frac{1}{3}\%$ was demanded by retailers and 40% by wholesalers. Normally such unreasonable demands were resisted but not for long as it became more and more apparent that the book trade could not be ignored. Mr Hambling was a marvellous, though toothless, customer, always friendly and encouraging and his model shop was nearly always overflowing with customers. I made frequent lunch hour sorties from Waterloo to collect his order and deliver his goods. W. H. Smith began to take a few more copies and I ventured into the sanctums of various bookstall managers who at the time were not the most cheerful of chappies. Most bookstalls were open to the elements and the manager had a minuscule 'office' about three feet square and was usually clad in overcoat, muffler and mittens. Waterloo Main was the first cold call and a fairly frosty reception, 'Why haven't you been before? I've been overwhelmed with people asking for these bloody books and didn't know where to get them from.' Waterloo Loop was more conciliatory and a cautious order was forthcoming. Victoria Continental had a manager who looked like a person-ification of Scrooge and took the sample book I proffered, scanned it for some minutes and gave it back saying 'It's just a list of bloody numbers, who do you think is going to buy this?' No order came forth. So I learnt the hard way how to be a salesman but it all became fun as we went along. Whilst W. H. Smith were friendly and accommodating, Wymans who ran the bookstalls on the GWR and LMS refused point blank to handle anything, presumably as their demands for 40% had been repulsed and despite the various letters and copies that had been sent.

Eventually I sought and obtained an interview with the book buyer, Bert Buddin, who was the toughest egg I had yet met. He snatched the specimen copy out of my hand and threw it on top of his cabinet saying 'That's where I throw all your books, I am fed up with amateur publishers who will not conform to standard trade practices and you can do what you like but you will not get an order from me until you do.' We talked and eventually he held out an olive branch: 'Give me my discount and I'll give you an order for 2,000 of each.' I nearly fell off the chair as I had only been dealing in dozens up till then. He got his terms and I got a super order. We ultimately became the best of friends.

Back at Waterloo, Grasemann who was a ship enthusiast hauled me in and said he would like to do a book on SR steamers called *Round the Southern Fleet* whilst Ben Webb also tried to get on the bandwaggon saying he had written a book *Fifty of the Famous — Musicians*. Well it was all good stuff to have the bosses writing for me and our little show was getting well on the road. So after the abc's and these other two diversions, what next?

A. B. MacLeod wanted to indulge himself on a book on *McIntosh Locomotives of the Caledonian Railway* which eventually appeared on that cream art paper which heralded the *abc of LMS Locomotives*. Uncle Mac had been rewarded: this highly expensive production at 3s 6d was really my thank you to him as it actually lost money and I began to realise that in publishing you don't win 'em all.

London Transport was my next target and totally uncharted land. I knew nothing whatever about tube stock, trams, trolleybuses or buses but I met a young Barrington Tatford, a pupil at Whitgift, who seemed to know it all. He produced the text and the pictures and this multi-stock book eventually appeared and, as was our wont, copies were sent for review to *Railway Gazette* and *Modern Transport* inter alia. This provoked a surprise. I was invited to lunch with the two then 'greats' of the transport journal scene, Charles E. Lee (Editor of *Railway Gazette*) and Charles Klapper (of *Modern Transport*). I looked forward to congratulations from such distinguished chaps but halfway through the soup, euphoria turned to anguish as they proceeded to pick the book to pieces page by page and made all sorts of nasty noises at me. Worse still, they went on carping long after my lunch hour was up and I was torn between listening to their catalogue of woe and the much more terrifying prospect of an irate chief clerk waiting to berate me for having two hours for lunch. Eventually I tore myself away with both of them demanding in strong terms that the book be withdrawn and all copies destroyed.

I decided to ignore them both. The book was a howling success and the 20,000 print was all gone in a few days. Lesson No 2 in publishing — often the books with the worst possible reviews are the best sellers and vice versa! Little did I think at the time of the 'roasting' I got from Klapper in the Aldwych Brasserie that he would one day become one of my employees, any more than when I placed the 5s 6d ad in *Railway World*, that the magazine would one day carry the Ian Allan imprint.

I believe I worked quite hard occasionally for the SR, as I had made it work hard for me. It had introduced me to a lot of people who had been so helpful, none more so than one of the secretaries of the GMO, Mollie Franklin. She did most of the typing of correspondence involved in laying the foundations of the publishing phenomenon which was beginning to happen. She was destined to become more, much more, involved.

It has been mentioned that these 'abc' books became used for marking off engines as they were seen and as the hobby grew, so did the problems. These came to a head in 1944 when a crowd of lads from Birmingham who had made the pilgrimage to Tamworth to watch trains on the LMS main line got bored when nothing was about so proceeded to place pennies on the main line to get them squashed by speeding 'Scots' and 'Duchesses'. Not surprisingly the railway management objected and set the police to work with the result that when the boys appeared in court so did the *abc of LMS Locomotives* about which the Beak had a few rude words to say.

In order to meet this problem a Club was formed to indoctrinate a code of good behaviour; all applicants for membership had to sign a declaration that they would not trespass on railway property. The 'ABC Locospotters' Club' had been formed and a new word coined into the English language — substantiated by the Encyclopaedia Britannica (junior version). The 'abc' was later dropped and a new badge designed incorporating in the then house style the name of 'Ian Allan'. And who to run the show? Why, Mollie Franklin of course. Having formed the Club and paid a whole 1s for the privilege, the membership started to demand action. Hence dozens of smaller groups were set up all over the country, all doing their own thing with meetings and shed visits, lectures and all the other things clubsters do.

# Train craze seizes boys of 6 and men of 90

**News Chronicle Reporter**

THE rage among boys for collecting train numbers is "sweeping the country," according to a police inspector giving evidence at a Tamworth juvenile court yesterday, when several Birmingham lads were accused of railway trespass.

During school holidays, he said, as many as 200 boys at a time went to Tamworth from places as far away as Bristol and Crewe, because it was an important rail centre crossed by two main lines.

They sometimes got out of hand, and to relieve boredom ran about the permanent way, putting pennies on the lines, which they afterwards collected as souvenirs.

*The club badge*

He added that a book had been issued with diagrams and descriptions of engines with columns for entering the types of locomotive observed

Yesterday I talked with the author of this "Spotters' ABC of Locomotives," which runs in a series of six booklets. He is a

**IAN ALLAN**
*Boys mob him*

man of 23, who works in the Southern Railway advertising office at Waterloo, and have name is Ian Allan.

In two years he has sold over 200,000 copies at 1s. and 2s. each, and he receives hundreds of letters daily from enthusiasts.

He told me that he was starting "spotters' clubs" all over the country and badges with club initials and a picture of an engine would be issued to members.

"Girls are becoming as keen as boys," he said, "and my correspondents range from boys of six to men of 90."

### Saturday sport

I saw forgetting myself on a children on Clapham Junction Station on a Saturday afternoon he said, "and have been mobbed for autographs on the way to my office.

"Many schoolmasters have formed spotters' clubs in their schools, and organised expeditions to railway junctions."

Mr. Allan, who is his own publisher, says he makes "quite a bit" out of his publications. Paper shortage is restricting his output, but he hopes to produce 20,000 copies a month.

*Harnessing the Southern to Work*

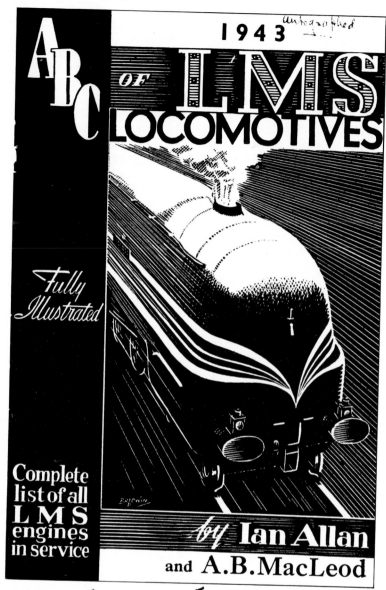

1943 *autographed*

**ABC** *of* **LMS LOCOMOTIVES**

*Fully Illustrated*

Complete list of all **LMS** engines in service

*by* **Ian Allan** and **A.B.MacLeod**

*Above:*
**The cover of the first LMS 'abc' kindly autographed within by William A. Stanier.**

*Left:*
**A clipping from the *News Chronicle* in 1944.**

This led on to great gatherings in London, Manchester, Birmingham and ultimately to excursions but a lot more water was to flow under the bridge before that state arrived. What the Tamworth incident did spark off was a great wave of publicity. A reporter from the *News Chronicle* buttonholed me and to my amazement a whole column appeared complete with a picture for which he had asked me to pose.

Other papers picked the story up so it did not really surprise me when the *Daily Mirror* 'phoned and asked me to visit them for a chat. Conscientiously I said it had to be during my lunch hour and I was invited to go hot foot on the morrow. I did not find myself in some newsroom or studio but in a panelled office where a distinguished looking chap introduced himself and invited me to sit. He asked all sorts of questions but took no notes which seemed a bit curious. 'How much do the railway people pay you?' he peremptorily asked. I told him it was about £2 a week. 'Come and work for the Daily Mirror and I'll start you at £9 10s.'

This was pay beyond the dreams of avarice for in those days I had set my sights on £500 a year as the ideal living wage which ultimately I could attain without working at all on the basis of 5% interest on £10,000, which had become my capital target figure. The chap I was talking to was none other than Cecil King, the Chairman of the *Mirror* who had beguiled me in on a recruitment drive. I said I'd think about it and departed though I knew I would not accept, even if he had offered me £90 a week. The Southern Railway and my budding business were far too dear to my heart.

Uncle Mac then had another of his bright ideas and up to Room 20 I was summoned, 'You must now start doing some proper casebound books.' The cost and the risk sounded horrific but he persisted and between us we settled on an idea for a book on all the named expresses on Britain's railways. 'Aristocrats of the Track' it nearly was until it was refined down to and published as *Titled Trains of Great Britain*. But who to write it? Mac was quite definite: 'Cecil J. Allen'. I was aghast, how could I — a lowly railway clerk — approach the great doyen of railway literature but duly directed I did and the great 'CJ' descended on me to my great embarrassment in the office at Waterloo and discussed the book at length and in fairly audible terms with my colleagues listening in. To my amazement he agreed to do it subject to acceptable 'remuneration'. There was no precedent. I had no experience of this sort of negotiation but tentatively suggested £200. It was accepted at once and moreover CJ vouchsafed that this was the highest offer he had ever received for a book — a shock (of bidding too high) from which I never recovered!

There had been lots of helpers — from Arthur Nicholls, who disappeared into the war and reappeared in the late 1980s, to Alistair MacLeod, Arthur

Baldwin, Bernard Anwell, O. J. Morris, Sidney Oborne and the army of distributors; now CJ had been roped in too. There was beginning to be a bit of an organisation and a bit of strength coming to it as well.

I enjoyed my days on the Southern. Working conditions were abysmal, the offices were never cleaned, the desks were always filthy as were the washroom and toilets. We sat at long desks — three aside — and opposite me was a rather run down chap whom I suspected did not wash too carefully or too often and I realised that in the warm weather there was a terrible smell wafting up from the direction of his feet. Not wanting to hurt his feelings and say anything, I put up with it. Then one day I decided to clean out a set of drawers which had previously been used by someone who had been called up. When I got to the bottom drawer I found in it two very large and very dead rats. My colleague's feet were proved innocent. The place was full of rats and mice who used to come each night and eat the spines off books and timetables. They obviously enjoyed the glue but selectively — Waterlow's books must have been very tasty and were gobbled up whilst those of McCorquodales were not such a rodent delicacy.

During my time on the Southern I made full use of the 'Staff Suggestion' scheme which for some curious reason was run by the *Southern Railway Magazine*. A form was provided with a perforated top on which the suggester's name and department were written, a special envelope was provided and as the numbered top was removed from the numbered bottom, complete anonymity was preserved. The suggestions came to the SRM, were readdressed to 'E. G. Trangmar Esq GMO' (one had to be very careful to address every one above the rank of Grade 1 Clerk as 'Esq' and below it 'Mr'). I was quite successful and was ceremonially awarded several cash prizes for pretty obvious proposals. In 1940 the Three Bridges—Bognor Regis off peak service was regularly operated as six-car (three x 2-BIL units) trains and carried as many passengers on a good day. My simple proposal to cut them down to four or two cars was hailed as Heaven sent inspiration and I was awarded £5 which was one month's salary! I cannot remember all the other brilliant ideas I had other than my *chef d'oeuvre* which won me no less than £25 and a commendation from the GM. Waterloo and one or two other stations had been fitted with the ON/OFF starting signal repeaters on the platforms with the 'ON' box being displayed for about 23¾ of every 24 hours. Fuel economy was the order of the day and I suggested the removal of the bulbs in the 'ON' boxes. Of course, nowadays these repeaters only have 'OFF' slots and I like to feel that goes back to my £25 winning proposal of 1944.

One suggestion I made landed me with a sound choking off from Ben Webb. The Publicity Department was the recipient of literally dozens of copies of *The Railway Gazette* each week which at 1s a go was a bit extravagant and they all came separately rolled and addressed. I suggested we cut our order down. I knew this was a bit of a touchy subject as the PRO department liked to keep in the good books of *RG* and *Modern Transport* — proverbial sunshine endlessly streaming from some part of their anatomies — so in order to circumvent the PRO chiefs I readdressed the envelope to the mystical 'E. G. Trangmar Esq' and sent it direct. Of course, when the topless suggestion came back for comment my writing was recognised and I was ticked off for 'meddling in politics'. I think I have always been a bit of a stink stirrer.

The war ended in 1945, my obligation to the nation to keep the wartime railways running ceased and I had to consider whether to take up private publishing or remain on course for the General Managership, though not much progress in that direction had been made other than that in seven years the remuneration package had risen from 15s to £2 15s 0d. A lot had been learned and a lot of friends made; I went to see Grasemann and asked his advice as to the way ahead to which his reply was brief and razor sharp: 'You'll be a bloody fool if you stay here.' Probably the decision had already been taken subconsciously but armed with that steer I tendered my resignation with regret and having cleared up my drawers and handed gently over to some returning soldier, I contemplated where next to go.

*Above:*
**A selection of early 'abc' jackets.**

# 3

# Forming the Company

The relief of waking up in the morning without the pressure of having to catch the 0824 was wonderful and the euphoria lasted for weeks as did the excitement of starting up a new business. Fortunately there was bags of help at hand, Uncle Tom was Treasury Solicitor and Cousin Jim was Chief Registrar in Bankruptcy thus Ian Allan Ltd was incorporated in a flash, in fact on 1 November 1945. At the time no self-respecting business could operate from anywhere but London and premises in London were somewhat hard to come by. However, next-door neighbour Frank Dommett (from 229 Laleham Road) who with his wife had stocked 'abcs' for some years and dealt with personal callers at 227 unable to get any reply, came up with a bright idea. He was trustee for a property near Victoria station more or less gutted by bomb damage but at least it had a roof and a war damage claim. The price of 282 Vauxhall Bridge Road was an astronomic £4,000 but he would agree to leaving £2,000 on mortgage at 4% simple interest. The deal was struck and Ian Allan Rubble Inc was initiated.

Now, amongst the army of collaborators at Waterloo was the Southern's official artist Arthur Baldwin who had produced the artwork for all the illustrated covers of the abc books to date. He was a wizard with the scraper board and duly overseen by the experts he had produced some most original and attractive designs. He was also somewhat disenchanted with life at Waterloo where he had been seconded from the GMO to 'Control' for the 'duration' notwithstanding that he had had no experience of railway operating and very little interest in it, so it never surprised me when 'Control', wherever it was, made a muck of things. He decided to leave and joined Ian Allan Ltd as 'development manager'; we also took on a super young secretary, Nancy Whitfeld, ex-Christ's Hospital office, who had just been demobbed from the Wrens.

We regarded the shambles of 282 and named it appropriately 'Mikado House'. It was a four storey building with a basement and a built-on front which was accessed by going down four steps. The whole of this front 'well' was rubble and the debris of four years of Victoria's rubbish. It was quite disgusting as was the building itself which had been freely available to all and sundry for years and all and sundry had most certainly used it. We nearly got off to a most disastrous start. Arthur Baldwin and I got to work with fairly elementary DIY equipment to make one or two rooms habitable but we hit a snag with the electrics which were non-existent. There was a £10 limit on expenditure on building repairs at the time but I had a good friend who was an electrician who offered to give us a hand. Meanwhile, the Estate Manager at Christ's Hospital offered to lend a couple of his chaps to do a spot of painting which all seemed quite legal to me as no-one was making any charge. So only the paint and very simplistic wiring material was involved and this really could have scraped (with some carefully constructive accounting) into the £10.

Alas, the building inspector from Westminster City Council decided to walk in when all six of us were hard at it and was not at all impressed when I explained that they were all 'my friends'. Perhaps I should have crossed his palm with silver, though this never occurred to me and I went cap in hand to the City Hall, where I was threatened with dire penalties, to enter my defence. Happily Christ's Hospital again came to the rescue. The Westminster surveyor lived at nearby Billingshurst and was a mate of the Estate Manager...and nothing more was heard!

*Above:*
**Vauxhall Bridge Road; the first office, the first desk and Margaret Brannagan trying hard to look businesslike.**

We had no furniture for even if we could have afforded it, there just was none to be bought. So with orange boxes for seats and a few basic essentials, publishing started in earnest from the heart of the City of Westminster — which sounded so much better than Vauxhall Bridge Road — and '282' was opposite the tram terminus so I spent many happy hours looking out of our newly glazed windows at the operation.

It was months before we could obtain a building licence to make the place properly habitable and the war damage claim settled for £780. But it was a wonderful start and the memory of Frank Dommett is honoured in the annals of the Company.

Now I would be wrong if I did not mention the great contribution of Willie Brett who had become an integral part of the operation. He had certainly moved up in the world since 1942 and whilst still with McCorquodales and engineering printing and paper for ongoing products, he was doing well out of his mail order sales. He gave great assistance and advice, especially on property matters in which he had quietly dabbled for years, and general buying and selling. He taught me all the things I should not have learnt but his shrewd judgement and counsel were of invaluable help to a developing business as, indeed, was the ongoing work provided by Mollie Franklin and her indefatigable typewriter.

Father, who had become Clerk of Christ's Hospital in 1936, retired in 1946 with an OBE and next day joined Ian Allan Ltd in a full-time capacity and was, of course, my great mentor; unlike Willie Brett, he taught me all the things I ought to know and do. He was a deeply committed Christian, a classicist, very well-read, bright at bookkeeping and had a strong literary bent and no business sense whatsoever having spent 57 of his 66 years in the cloistered calm of Christ's Hospital.

282 Vauxhall Bridge Road was a tall thin building in a terrace of three squashed between Denison House and a dilapidated building in the centre of the Victoria 'red light' district. It had a semi-basement, two small rooms on the ground floor repeated on the other two floors but with better rooms at lst floor level with large Georgian windows from floor to ceiling; it faced south and was virtually unbearable in the summer. After refurbishment I took the first floor front and Father the first floor back. We had one toilet on the stairs between us all. The basement remained uninhabitable as did the garage at the rear as the building licence did not stretch to refurbishing these and they remained insanitary rubbish dumps for some months.

On retirement my parents moved from Staines to Brighton, a move I greatly regretted; 225/7 Laleham Road was a super house in two acres of garden and I was very sad. The much vaunted one hour journey from Victoria to

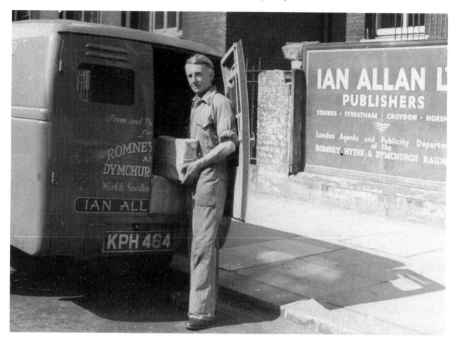

*Above:*
**Outside 282 Vauxhall Bridge Road in 1946 one of our first employees, George Betteridge, loads our brand new Ford van whilst in the background can be seen the bomb damaged boarded-up premises.**

Brighton soon proved a myth as the trains were never punctual in the rush hour. Joining a No 7 to Roedean, it took two hours each way and I soon got fed up with it and bored with Brighton. So in concert with Willie Brett and my cousin John Cannon, we decided to buy some shop premises and start a model shop in Brighton. Brett had always been a frequenter of Brighton and John Cannon's 'Uncle Fred' of Southdown lived and worked in the town so we had a good base to start on and we bought some tatty shop premises at 34 Queen's Road, a hundred yards or so from the station. Fortuitously our names fell immediately into ABC Models from the company name Allan Brett Cannon Ltd. It was a long hard grind getting anything to sell and much time was spent scanning the classified ads of local rags to find people with model railways to sell. Our first client was Cecil J. Allen who had a superb outdoor gauge 0 layout and who had decided he had now grown out of it. We learnt our first lesson in selling it on the basis of prewar prices and found too late to our chagrin how much we *could* have made if we had been aware of the shortage value.

Back at 282 business was brisk and we were rapidly running out of space; however, the building licence arrived and we built the front into a shop and the area behind it into a packing room. Allan Brett Cannon took the shop on board and despatches of books happened from the nether regions and garage and the local postman was kept very busy. Then one day perched on a stool in the 'Windsor Castle' having a quick lunchtime bite, I found myself sitting next to someone from the SR Estate Department with whom I had had some contact during the war at 'Sitka'. He appeared interested in our developments and asked whether I would like the top of an arch at London Bridge.

Hot foot the place was inspected, it would obviously make a large shop and at £4 a week it seemed reasonable. The deal was struck and a builder went in to erect a shop front only to report that the floor was lined with thick lead on which batteries had been stored and worth quite a packet. I reported back to the Estate Department who really did not want to know and declared that we had taken the premises over and so we could do what we liked with them. The value of the lead paid for most of the shop front — a small instance of the serendipity and good luck with which I have been blessed in most, but not all, of my business life. The shop went to Allan Brett Cannon as their No 3 branch whilst the rear premises, directly over what is now the London Dungeon, became the Ian Allan Ltd warehouse and distribution centre.

This shop opened about the time that Graham Farish launched his first train sets on the market: we set up a great relationship and sold hundreds of his unusual tender-driven locos — and when he gave up model railways for fibreglass dinghies, John Cannon and I bought one each and enjoyed them till once, far out at sea, a hole appeared in the bottom and we began to sink. Fortunately we were both good swimmers and not only made the shore ourselves, actually brought the boat back too.

On the publishing front there had been several developments: there was a demand for postcards, something which had disappeared during the war but these carried purchase tax which made invoicing very difficult so we struck on the idea of collecting some postcard size pictures and printing them in book form. The first *Titans of the Track* was a random collection of pickings I had gathered from some of the stalwarts who had supplied photographs to illustrate the 'abcs' such as H. C. Casserley and M. W. Earley. This book was easy enough to produce and proved a reasonable seller. It was quickly followed by others and were, of course, the precursors of the *My Best Railway Photographs* series which followed later. We were already publishing London Transport 'abcs' and it was a natural follow on to look at bus and aircraft subjects. Uncle Fred was approached at Southdown, meanwhile an author was sought for an 'abc' of Airliners, later to become the regular *Civil Aircraft Markings*. Owen Thetford was the first compiler and later a long and lasting friendship was established with John W. R.-

Taylor who took over the job. We went into partnership with Ron Warring and Bill Dean, two leading exponents of model aircraft, and produced *Model Aeronautics*. Alas, like so many other things we pioneered at the time, we were too 'young' to give them the attention they needed and regretfully we pulled out and a great publishing opportunity was lost.

We also had an amusing sortie with Christmas cards which were in very short supply. Baldwin had produced some rather nice pen-and-ink sketches of cathedrals. We managed to get a printer to work on them and obtained orders for the lot. They were delivered to us on 20 December and we had to distribute them around London pronto. We had no van but Farmer John Cannon came to the rescue with his farm trailer hitched to the rear of his milk sodden prewar Hillman Minx. He and I set off. We delivered our loads unwrapped and liberally decorated with cow pats and other similar substances. We were booked for driving an unauthorised trailer in Hyde Park and on the way home down the Great West Road were stopped for speeding (although there was then no restriction) because the trailer appeared dangerous. The two coppers were suspicious of the trailer and obviously assumed that we were nicking turkeys, a theory they thought they had confirmed for when they asked us what we were doing with a farm trailer at high speed; the answer 'delivering Christmas cards' seemed a bit thin. John was fined £1 and I split the cost with him.

The development of book publishing is a never-ending saga but I can say that in those early days I had no idea of costing and practically everything we did lost money except the 'abcs' which sold in such prodigious quantities that their profits covered up the other losses, alas to the extent that in those early years we were only just about breaking even. I was suffering the legacy of my first bank manager who had saddled me with an accountant who gave me no help whatsoever and merely put the end of year numbers together. At this time he was well into his 80s, always appearing in a butterfly collar, black jacket, waistcoat and striped trousers: on one occasion he felt benevolent and invited me to a formal accountants' dinner in the City warning me that dinner dress was the appropriate attire. I duly turned up in a dinner jacket with an evening shirt with attached, turned-down collar. He, of course, had a boiled shirtfront and wing collar. He eyed me disapprovingly for the whole evening and eventually could contain himself no longer. 'What exactly are you wearing?' he demanded. I explained that my outfit was generally considered acceptable nowadays to which he gruffly replied 'Well *I* don't like it.' Soon after he went to the great Chartered Accountants' hall in the sky and I inherited his assistant who took over the account, Charles Roy Knevitt Mace, who, young at the time, took me under his wing and gave good advice in those early pioneering days when he was co-partner in a small accountancy practice.

*Above:*
**An Ian Allan trade dinner in 1948. Left to right: standing George Allan, Terry Holder, A. B. MacLeod, Frank Harding, an eclipsed Ian Allan, J. Baumber (WHS), Sam Brown (McCorquodales), O. J. Morris, Bert Buddin (Wymans), A. Minshull (Simpkin Marshall) and, in the right foreground, Willie Brett.**

*Left:*
**Arthur Baldwin and Terry Holder.**

Meanwhile, the Locospotters' Club had developed and had enrolled thousands of members, though, of course, new chaps came in and others left, but we always claimed as membership everyone who had ever enrolled and used it as a valuable publicity medium. This brought an enquiry from one Terence J. Holder (Major RE Retd), manager of the Romney Hythe & Dymchurch Railway. His initial approach was for parties to be brought down to ride his newly reopened railway. I say 'his' but thereby hangs a tale. The railway belonged to J. E. P. Howey, whose wife Gladys played a leading role in running the show. They were both somewhat jealous of Terry Holder's vibrant personality and did their best to emphasise that it was not Terry's railway and that he was not even General Manager but 'the Manager'. Terry put up with quite a lot of stick from the Howeys who he said only considered that he was working when he was filthy dirty driving a train.

We had great fun with the RH&DR and we became very attached to it. Ian Allan Ltd were appointed publicity agents and Arthur Baldwin who had family contacts in the area played a leading part in getting the act together. I was highly flattered and chuffed at such an appointment with so famous a concern that all other considerations — like doing it profitably — went out of the window. Terry was demanding. Laurel and Hardy were appearing at the Palladium and he wanted them down to open the 1946 season. I did not believe it possible but we tried and were almost immediately in the dressing room at the Palladium consuming giant glasses of whisky, which I couldn't — and still cannot — stand and discussing the details. It was on: a deal was struck, they would appear and do the honours and all for free provided we could get newsreel coverage. We could and we did. They were superb and played to the cameras and the audience magnificently, the mayor was there and all the crowned heads of Romney Marsh.

So successful was the publicity that Terry demanded more for next year. Tommy Handley and the 'ITMA' gang were still top of the radio pops and they all agreed to come down. We talked coach operators Timpsons into providing a vehicle which they not only did but provided Mr Timpson as

*Above:*
**Laurel and Hardy at New Romney in 1946 with the Mayor and a rather youthful Terry Holder and Ian Allan dressed with sartorial elegance in his best mackintosh.**

well who entertained the whole company at a watering hole en route which he happened to own. We repeated the performance the following year and the RH&DR were well and truly on the map.

The years from 1945 to 1952 spanned the period of our sojourn at 282. The Company had four directors — my father and I, O. J. Morris and Cecil J. Allen. 'OJ' was a staunch Roman Catholic; Cecil was an even more staunch non-conformist so we had to eat fish on Fridays whilst the mere mention of alcohol or any Sunday activity sent 'CJ' into apoplexy. CJ was not an easy bedfellow but he had many good qualities and was well-known in many spheres. First he introduced his son Geoffrey Freeman who had just been demobbed and was looking for career prospects. Whether or not he wanted to come to Ian Allan Ltd I know not, but no doubt persuaded by his father he did and very quickly absorbed the necessary know-how and became an invaluable part of the new company. His first job was to translate Jack Howey's photo album of the construction of the RH&DR into a 1s 6d. book entitled *The Line that Jack Built* and thereby commenced a close connection which lasted for 25 years. Arthur Baldwin joined the Board and GFA became Company Secretary in succession to Cousin Jim who felt that as Registrar in Bankruptcy his position as Secretary could be embarrassing should he ever have to summon himself to Carey Street and wind himself up. GFA also took on the role of book producer.

In 1946 I thought it was time we produced a journal, *The Locomotive, Railway Magazine* and *Railway World* had had it all their own way and I was anxious to compete. Paper restriction prohibited new periodicals and I assumed that random undated publications would be OK. To determine policy and to round up help I assembled a meeting comprising O. J. Morris and CJA, Rixon Bucknall, H. C. Casserley, Maurice Earley, one or two others, my father and me. He offered me the Court Room at the Christ's Hospital office in Great Tower Street, a formidable panelled room covered in portraits of the illustrious: my panel too was formidable. Rixon Bucknall was a colonel in the Guards and the others well-known figures. As a callow 24-year old, I jibbed at taking the chair but was forced into it by my parent — my first public meeting. Amazingly it went well and a policy and promises of help duly came forth. I should have expected it for everyone in those early days was bubbling over with good will. We launched *Trains Illustrated* at the Holborn Restaurant with a 5s (that being the maximum legal cost of a meal) dinner and due celebration amongst our contributors, printers and trade friends. The 100 x 5s bill finished up about 10 times this price as the 'trade' and other friends had very dry throats to lubricate and such lubrication was unrestricted pricewise. No 1 duly appeared with a blessing from my former General Manager at Waterloo, Sir Eustace Missenden, who wrote the Foreword, and by input from O. J. Morris and U. A. Vincent who had appeared somewhere down the line from the LMS and unofficially

*Above:*
**U. A. Vincent behind the stand at a Model Railway Club exhibition in the early 1950s.**

attached himself to us. Editing a magazine and building a business proved too much and CJ did not approve of my style, or O. J. Morris's, anyway. He offered to edit *Trains Illustrated* and did so for the next few issues until the Paper Controller rumbled us and said 'No more'. Fortunately the restrictions almost immediately lifted and we proceeded to a monthly basis and from strength to strength with CJ handing over to GFA after a year or so. The circulation rose from my initial 13,500 (all the paper I could scrounge) to well over 70,000 in its heyday. It was, indeed, a little acorn from which a mighty oak tree grew.

CJA was, of course, the doyen of train timing and locomotive performance reportage – a subject on which I contributed occasionally to his disgust. I had a ride up once with Driver Bill Till on the 'Devon Belle' which he took over at Wilton. He certainly gave a magnificent performance getting the speed up to over 92mph which was fairly well over the top in those days. So much so that one of the ancient Pullmans was unable to stand the pace and almost caught fire. CJA was a God-fearing chap who never used expletives — until he read my article — when he summed it all up with 'Bloody!' mainly I think because *I* had written on his sacred territory and was probably not as accurate as his stop-watch timings would have been.

Bill Till retired that day and joined us as a packer and was great at public gatherings with boys and girls.

The early days of the company at 282 Vauxhall Bridge Road were exciting. It was difficult to find paper and decent printers but I was not really in business. It was all very much a hobby and I had never — contrary to popular opinion — thought of making my publishing activity a profitable business. As long as I could recover costs I was happy.

The big event in 1947 was that after growing the Locospotters' Club and looking after much of my business affairs for years, Mollie Franklin decided that she had better marry me and make an honest man of me. I concurred and have been concurring ever since! Receptions in 1947 were hard to come by but Arthur Baldwin had a relative — 'Uncle Ari', a Greek *maître d'hôtel* running the Lansdowne Restaurant in Berkeley Square, who offered to look after us — and well he did after the wedding at nearby St George's, Hanover Square, where my uncle, the Vicar of Alborne, Sussex, did the honours, assisted by the Rector of Sutton to whom my father had been Churchwarden and who prepared me for confirmation. It was a great day followed by a honeymoon in Scotland et al visiting all the railway hotels I could find. I have never lived down the fact that one night of aforesaid honeymoon was spent in the Midland Hotel, Manchester and one in the Central Hotel, Glasgow!

We bought a small house by the river at Laleham midway between Staines and Shepperton and settled down to married bliss. I had always loved swimming and boats so our position was ideal: pollution had not then been invented and from a landing stage constructed (naturally) out of railway sleepers, I was able to have a daily — sometimes twice daily — dip in the Thames and a small sailing dinghy in which I spent most of my time either becalmed or totally out of control.

Apart from the development of a publishing company, Allan Brett Cannon was becoming quite a force in the model railway world and I was attempting a few print-farming jobs in conjunction with the various printers with whom I had built up a good rapport. Some of these were profitable and some were certainly not. Willie Brett rang me from McCorquodales one day and said he had a large order for Southern Railway season tickets which they could not handle and could I/would I take it on and farm it out: the job was urgent and cost was not of great import. It *seemed* a licence to print money. So we took on the job and hit two immediate snags, firstly no printer wanted to touch it, printing on heavy card was not practical for most of the machines and secondly, the tiny runs and minute variations of the tickets made the job most tedious and complicated.

I used every persuasive tactic I could muster and eventually got the job done. Masses of tickets arrived at 282 Vauxhall Bridge Road. The weekly seasons were of different material from the monthlies and three monthlies; for each destination there were first and third class varieties and some with varying routes so that for instance a simple Chertsey-Waterloo season came in something like six varieties. U. A. Vincent, who although I knew him well for many years never divulged his Christian name, came over from Euston for several days and nights and we sorted the whole shooting match out on the threadbare carpet of my room. We delivered on time but were never asked to quote again — and never would have even if we had been!

This was just one of the many hare-brained schemes which seemed good at the time but which were in fact mini financial disasters. Like the now rapidly developing Locospotters' Club, which Mollie and her hard-working mother had been running until Mrs H. C. Casserley took it on board and with gusto and enthusiasm started to make it all happen. Visits and rallies abounded and a circus team of myself, Baldwin and Casserley perambulated the country or staged rallies at Dennison House next door to us at 282. These were attended by anything from 300 to 400 avid spotters and entertained by CJA, O. J. Morris and other accomplished lecturers, by film shows, slide shows and, of course, tea and buns. The charges were supposed to cover our costs but they never did; the hidden overheads always swamped the revenue but we were all too naive and enthusiastic to notice it. I think it was all a personal ego trip and I rather enjoyed the glory of it all and the masses of autographs I signed.

The next step, of course, was to do something big — a visit to Swindon Works. Much to my surprise the GWR (or was it BR WR by then?) agreed both to the visit and to running a special train. This was the first postwar enthusiast special and was the forerunner of the hundreds which were subsequently run under the Ian Allan headboard and that of many others. The train ran non-stop to Swindon and incorporated a restaurant car on which tea was provided consisting of a pot of tea, toasted tea cake and sandwiches. I remember remonstrating hard at the exorbitant charge of 3s 8d and to placate me a chocolate biscuit was included in the deal.

Thereafter we ran trip after trip to railway workshops at Eastleigh, Derby, Doncaster, Horwich: you name it, we went there and were usually allowed

*Above:*
**SR driver Bill Till unfolding the mysteries of engine driving to a youthful audience.**

*Below:*
**Laurie Earl, an ex-LMS top link driver, was a great supporter of the Locospotters' Club and is seen here investing the 100,000th member, Ralph Owen, with an outsize badge.**

*Above:*
**What must have been one of the first rail excursions after the war. The platform party at Waterloo beside 'Merchant Navy' *Elders Fyffes*: with George Drury, Arthur Streatfield (PRO), Stationmaster Matthews and the famous John Pelham Maitland, Shedmaster at Nine Elms — note his outsize boots.**

*Below:*
**An early Locospotters' Club Special waiting to depart from Waterloo.**

to select our choice of locomotive. These were simple trips but nevertheless the precursors of the more complicated affairs which followed in the 1960s. They were all money losers but great publicity gimmicks and were always good for editorial mention in the national and local press.

One was even a money loser for BR for on the return journey we stopped at Grantham where there was a goods train on the adjoining line, one of our bright young lads managed to lean out of the window and pull the pin holding a side flap from an open wagon: this fell open leaning against our train. As we set off the wagon 'flap' gently ripped all the door handles and other hardware off the entire train. Happily BR did not send us the bill but did rather bitterly advise of the cost!

The railway brotherhood was beginning to develop and people like P. B. Whitehouse, Eric Treacy, P. Ransome-Wallis, C. C. B. Herbert were starting to stick their heads up above the parapet. Treacy was then a vicar in Edgehill, Liverpool, Ransome-Wallis a doctor at Herne Bay, Herbert a railwayman with masses of photographs. One day Pat Whitehouse invited me to go with him and our wives to Ireland to explore the Tralee & Dingle and County Donegal Railways. We agreed to meet at Fishguard in our respective cars whence he said we should sail to Waterford. I booked our passage as instructed and duly arrived at Fishguard in the late evening in a howling gale to find the Waterford steamer was a diminutive prewar cattle ship — mostly full of cattle and smelling pretty high. There was no sign of the Whitehouses who eventually showed up after car loading (by crane) had finished and we assumed they had missed the boat. 'Oh no' said Whitehouse nonchalantly, 'We didn't want to travel on that cattle-ship. We are booked on the Rosslare boat' with a gesture pointing to the massive *St Patrick* which looked like an ocean liner compared with our poor little steamer. We had a lousy crossing and had to wait hours in Waterford for the advent of our almost ex-friends. After that we had a good holiday and some years later got our own back when our car broke down in France and they had to tow us home. What a pity the Tralee & Dingle and County Donegal closed soon after our visit.

It is interesting to see how all these railway 'names' with many others persisted throughout the years and became quite a fraternity which exists until this day. A lot of it started at the top end of Vauxhall Bridge Road when in those rationed days it was difficult to get a decent meal; chicken was a delicacy and steak was impossible. But not for us, we found this friendly restaurant which CJA, OJM and the rest of us frequented and where I first met Treacy. We always enjoyed a tender steak. One day OJ opted for fish which was surprising as it was not a Friday; he had his usual dollop of mustard with it for he ate mustard with everything. Asked why he was not taking advantage of the steak, he pointed to a notice on the wall which we had

*Above:*
**Crowding into the train for Doncaster are some of the lads who were delayed on the return journey when the train was severely damaged at Grantham by the removal of a pin from the flap of an adjacent goods train.**

*Below:*
**Inside the beaver-tail of the LNER observation car. Ian Allan seems to be pointing out something but no-one seems to be paying very much attention to him, especially his wife who seems more interested in Alan Pegler.**

never seen before 'Horseflesh only served in this restaurant'. We were stopped in our tracks and I felt sick for a week. What an extraordinary thing prejudice is and we never went there again. As now, lots of those early nuts were fairly odd. There was nothing normal about O. J. Morris or Sidney Oborne, Hamilton Ellis and many others probably including me. I dreaded having to meet them in their homes where stale food, stale tobacco and a goodly dust encrustation — even on the crockery — was the order of the day. O what I suffered for the company.

Not only did a railway fraternity grow up but one of our printers and block-makers. I used a firm in Islington — H. O. Lloyd & Co — who had printed the *Southern Railway Magazine* and with whom I renewed contact after I left Waterloo. Theirs was a primitive but friendly letterpress factory and I got to know Bob Lloyd who ran the place and his colleague, Wilson Mox-ham, who happened to live opposite Basil Gibbs in St Albans, who ran Gibbs & Bamforth and the *Herts Advertiser*. I had been introduced to him by CJA as Basil printed *The Crusader*, a Christian journal which CJ edited. We all became good friends and were invited by Bob Lloyd to join him on a steamer trip from Southend. The GSNCo had just put *The Royal Daffodil* back into service and it cruised out of Southend, or rather off the 1½-mile long pier, at 0930 daily in the summer and over to Margate and 'off the French coast' as international conditions still made landing on the Conti-nent a complicated affair. We were welcomed aboard by the Captain and invited to the bridge for coffee but asked to leave whilst departure took place; on our return at 0935 the duty free gin bottle was on the table and the day's work began. I have never been seasick but I do remember leaving Margate and lying down on a bench in the stern of the boat and watching the masts waving about in the air and feeling like death. I resolved to be more careful in future and beware of the dreaded ship's gin bottle. This trip became an annual event and, though the shipping line, personnel and venues have all changed, subsists until the present day.

From this trip evolved an annual outing to France: there were 10 of us to start with and they were all printers, blockmakers, paper merchants and others of that ilk. It was always hilarious and we all had never-to-be-repeated experiences. We transferred our affections from the GSNCo to BR when they introduced their 55s day trip from Victoria to Boulogne. The boat train had a Pullman Car and Frank Harding, the Pullman GM, would book our party in for breakfast on the way down and dinner on the return trip. The train left at 0900 and breakfast finished by about 0930. By 0945 the first tots of alcohol were beginning to flow. After a few years we began to know our way around — we thought. We had found a friendly taxi driver called Marcelle who would drive us for lunch at Wimereux and bring us back in time for the 17.15 return ship; on one occasion we arrived back at about 1705 to find the ship had sailed and no more scheduled services that day. Our remonstrations were met by reference to a sign stating that ships would sail up to 15 minutes before time if they were ready to go. Some of the party were highly alarmed and started handing out 10s notes like confetti to bribe their way home. We were lucky, there was a party of 750 women from West Hartlepool travelling on a special boat and we rather sheepishly joined them but alas, their connecting trains were running non-stop to the other side of London. More 10s notes and it was agreed that a stop be made at Bickley to let us off.

One night we came back on the bridge of the *Invicta*, the 'Golden Arrow' ship; the captain was fairly well-oiled and we sailed astern into the harbour arm at Folkestone at an angle of about 45° and hit it with an almighty bump. 'Bit of a rough shunt' we commented to the cox'n who unemotionally replied 'Actually he's better than usual tonight.'

From those trips we brought home various goodies for our wives who were fairly impressed. At least we usually got ourselves home — but not always. One of our printers, Reg Stone, managed to have an accident on a go-cart at Le Touquet, broke three ribs and ruined his suit but dared not tell his wife. On another occasion he got in the train at Charing Cross and agreed that his wife should meet him at Gravesend: he went to sleep and woke up at Strood. He returned to Gravesend by the next train whilst his wife guessing what had happened, drove to Strood and they never met. And at some time most of us have returned minus pants, false teeth, passports and other appendages. We are all older and wiser now and resort decorously merely to the Isle of Wight.

In publishing we developed a few simple standards. All the paperbacks were 6in x 4in with 64 pages, a card cover printed in three colours and we printed 10,000 copies. The cost was about £230 so I had a simple task of tossing each new project to two or three printers and play one against the other, often finishing up tossing a coin for the odd £10 and I almost always won. It was all very friendly and there was a virtually guaranteed market; we knew we could always sell 90% of the print run and in those days it was more difficult to obtain the goods anywhere near time than it was to sell them.

# 4

# Building the Business

One day in 1948, Terry Holder came into the office at Vauxhall Bridge Road and intimated that he had been fired as manager of the RH&DR; he did not say as much but he must have given a broad hint of his availability and I invited him to become our sales manager. I couldn't believe my luck when he accepted; here was a high powered dynamic bloke coming into a very embryonic business and I have no hesitation in saying that it was he who made us into a recognised publishing house. He was the greatest salesman I ever met, his enthusiasm would enable him to sell almost anything to anyone though he often left others to clean up the mess he left behind. Selling was his forte, administration was not.

*Above:*
**An early shop window display. One of Terry Holder's first innovations.**

But before he left Romney I had become reasonably friendly with both Jack and Gladys (the 'Dragon') Howey which led to an understanding that I was likely — at a price to be agreed — to fall heir to the RH&DR. Jack Howey was very rich and had a penchant for collecting expensive toys like motor cars and miniature locomotives and his house was festooned with trophies, one of which was a beautiful 10¼in gauge 'Royal Scot' which sat in the dining room fireplace.

With Terry's help he set this up on the beach at Hastings with a deal with Hastings Corporation. After a season he got bored with it and decided to sell it all. Five other chaps and I decided to form a consortium to raise the necessary asking price of £4,000 reduced to £3,500 on negotiation. Thus I became a one-sixth owner of a railway and Hastings Miniature Railway came into being, the other five being Fred Cannon (of Southdown), John Cannon, Willie Brett, Basil Gibbs and my father — a weird assortment who quite soon whittled down to just Allan, Brett and Cannon with Jim Hughes as manager. Jim Hughes was another 'one off'. We met him through his brother Charles our ABC Ltd manager: their father was a signalman at Byfleet where they all lived close to the SR main line. They were all live steam model enthusiasts and had a 3½in gauge line in their small garden and a super little tank engine called *Jabberwok* on which I and several others received basic driving and engineering training. When Jim went to Hastings the whole family up anchored and went with him to work on the Hastings Miniature Railway.

Terry always steered me towards obtaining the RH&DR from the Howeys and I had discussions with them both as to my acquiring it after he had reached the 'permanently horizontal' position as I tactfully tried to put it to him. It was agreed that we should have first refusal when the time came.

Terry Holder revolutionised our selling techniques. He took our pride and joy, our 10cwt Ford van, and had it fitted with movable shelves like a baker's. He then loaded up his wares and guaranteed that if he could get a bookstall manager out to see what he had we could sell him his needs and deliver it on the spot. He would go off for a fortnight at a time, 'phoning in for fresh supplies once or even twice a day. We would then rush parcels to the appropriate London terminals and fire them down by passenger train for him to collect at a designated station. In this way he soon had our sales graph soaring. He would force me out to go visiting with him and between us we built up a network of selling points throughout the country where we knew we were always welcome as we had a product which we knew the whole trade was crying out for.

In those heady far off days, selling and buying techniques in the trade were very different from today's computer-ridden impersonal transactions. I first met Joe Hoyles when he was manager of W. H. Smith's bookstall at Lewes where we did some business but not much so I was very pleased when he was transferred to Waterloo Main and quickly became not only my 'godfather' but my best customer. He was a law entirely to himself, he was far beyond WHS's management and did so well that like many other local managers in those days, he was left to run his own ship. All business was transacted in the Long Bar on the station, all reps and other sellers had to be on parade by 11am when it opened: Mr Hoyles liked his glass of port, though when I say 'glass' I mean glasses. Orders came forth about 2pm and someone had then to buy his lunch; there was always a large drinking entourage and everyone had to stand his round and anyone who seemed to be fairly slow to put his hand in his pocket was quickly spotted and Joe would command that 'odd man out' bought the next round. This was done by drawing a coin from the pocket and exposing it head or tails, though everyone except the victim would be warned which way to show the coin and eventually the heel tapper was caught.

A different technique was operated at Victoria where orders depended on how many 'overs' came with each delivery. I remember the manager telling me one day that he had agreed a special bank holiday weekend display of some new paperback. 'I ordered 1,000 copies,' he said, 'and they delivered 1,000 so they all went under the counter and were returned unsold, undisplayed on the Tuesday.' No doubt a salutory warning to me.

But you can be embarrassed by oiling wheels with a little bribery and corruption. Bert Buddin, the buyer at Wymans, had no scruples at all in accepting anything from hard cash to lunches, bottles of wine, you name it and he'd take it: one year he even asked for a greenhouse as a Christmas present. So when he retired and his assistant took over, the great quandary was whether he'd expect the same treatment. I thought not but my selling aides persuaded me that he would be upset if his palm was not duly crossed with the folding stuff as had his predecessor been. Fool that I was, I accepted their advice and my offer was very politely but very very firmly rejected. I was totally embarrassed and never did the like again.

But a growing business without much experience and perhaps too much enthusiasm can bring problems as many people obviously find out. I met my first Waterloo in 1950 when we started to run out of money. During the four years since 1946 we had made a lot of profit out of 'abcs' and I suspect lost most of it on spotters' excursions and unprofitable publishing enterprises and I learnt dramatically the maxim which we now put in every office in our Group: 'Turnover means nothing, it's the profit that counts.' Willie Brett rang me from McCorquodales one afternoon to say 'I'm with our accountant and he says you owe £2,500, would you put a cheque in the post.' I replied 'You know jolly well we haven't got a penny,' to which he responded obviously for cosmetic purposes, 'Many thanks, we'll look forward to receiving it.' Within five minutes Basil Gibbs came on with exactly the same message and coincidentally for exactly the same amount with a slightly different delivery, 'You've had the goods old boy, now pay up!' I turned to my beloved father and asked where we could get £5,000 from, thinking he might have a few thousand knocking about. To my surprise he replied, 'I've got no money, never have had but don't worry, something will turn up.' Well, I did worry but something did turn up — Willie Brett who produced a cheque for £850 from his own account; John Cannon coughed up £500 and next day Terry had the simple solution — go round to W. H. Smith and ask them to advance some money. Now W. H. Smith always remitted on the 21st of the month and on this occasion it was the 1st and I did not think there was a hope of screwing anything out of a big organisation just like that. I was wrong, I called on the magazine buyer, A. V. Harris, and told him my plight. He listened sympathetically and said, 'Hang on, I'll see if I can get one of the partners to sign a cheque.' Five minutes later he appeared with £1,500 in his hand. So with help like that and a bit of sharper credit control the debts were paid off and I resolved not to get in that mess again. As Willie put it so rightly, 'That little experience will be worth five figures to you,' and it was.

In fact so much so that by 1951 we were looking for bigger premises, the Vauxhall Bridge Road/London Bridge operation was completely swamped and although 282 had done a little marriage broking we decided to look elsewhere. The romances were firstly Nancy Whitfeld who married Brian Eves, a school friend of mine who had been demobbed and acted as a rep for us pending his return to his civilian job and Geoffrey Allen who married a girl who came as my secretary and later took him over — Gertrude Mary Newman — Gertie to me; Mary to him.

I had spotted a large house at Hampton Court with a For Sale board — only seven miles from Laleham — and thought how nice it would be not to have to come to London every day and to avoid the mounting traffic and parking problems. Craven House had been on the market for some time and we negotiated with the agent an offer of £7,000 for this large Georgian edifice complete with stable block and ostler's cottage. The offer was unacceptable and the vendor decided to go to auction and we instructed the agent to bid up to £7,500. In the event we got it for £6,500 which pleased me no end. We started to plan our move when we hit the first stumbling block — Defence Regulation 68(c)(a), a formula which is etched in my mind. This was the forerunner of planning regulations and forbade the use of residential property for commercial purposes without consent from the local authority. We duly applied and were turned down and the £6,500 bargain began to look more like a very expensive white elephant.

*Above:*
**'Craven House', Hampton Court soon after purchase.**

*Right:*
**Hilda Harmer giving driving lessons to Paul Allan. These were so effective that he became chairman of a motor company.**

Our solicitor recommended the best counsel for an appeal and duly briefed Derek Walker-Smith (later destined for higher things) who twisted the Clerk and Surveyor of Twickenham Council up in knots and the Inspector found in our favour. The way was clear but the consent only stretched to the ground and first floors. Which was fine. We made a caretaker's flat at the top, turned the stable into a packing store and prepared to move.

Sadly my father who had helped throughout the negotiations and, indeed, had been a mainstay of the business since 1942 suddenly collapsed and died within a week at the age of 72 and my world temporarily disintegrated.

During our sojourn at 282 Terry Holder had recruited as my secretary following the translation of G. M. Newman to GFA's nest on the top floor, the redoubtable Miss Harmer. Hilda Harmer was a formidable woman. She had been a LBSCR ticket collector in World War 1; later joined the Pullman Car Co and risen to be secretary to the MD and had, I believe, had a pretty free hand in bossing everyone around until the arrival of the new General Manager, Frank Harding, after World War 2.

The chemistry did not mix and when HH's remuneration remained at £5 10s a week and a new girl half her age was appointed at £6, she upped and moved across Vauxhall Bridge Road and started to run Ian Allan Ltd.

Frank Harding was so pleased with Terry at getting her off his back that he gave him a Pullman Free Pass on the spot.

Miss Harmer was a great tower of strength and though she lived at Selhurst was quite happy to move to Hampton Court where she quickly took up the reins of the accountant's job my father's sudden death had left vacant. She was the world's greatest messer, her desk and cupboard were so untidy it seemed impossible for anyone to work efficiently in such conditions. But she did, and knew where everything was and could find any paper in 30 seconds flat. Nothing got past her, her credit control was second to none: she worked all hours of the day and night and it soon became the accepted fact that if you were in with her you were all right. If not, you could start looking for another job. GFA and I were always, well almost always, in her good books, Arthur Baldwin and many others were not and they went, a process which continued until her eventual retirement some 25 years later.

Ian Allan Ltd had had a long association with the Locomotive Publishing Co of 88 Horseferry Road — an old established company run previously by A. R. Bell and W. G. Tilling, a couple of real old railway nutters and at this time managed by one Charles Simpson, an engineer by profession and a very decent chap. He had scant business acumen and there were clashes when his organisation (sic) failed to deliver. One day he came into the office sadly saying, 'I feel a degree of acrimony is creeping into our correspondence.' That was true but he was such a nice man one could not be cross with him especially as in admitting his shortcomings he invited us to buy the Loco Pub Co lock, stock and barrel: this included the monthly *Locomotive, Carriage and Wagon Review*, 25,000 glass negatives going back to the year dot and all the stock including the F. Moore postcard plates. We did a deal even retaining Simpson to edit *The Locomotive* on our behalf. We moved all the stock to Hampton Court and directed the removal team to put all the photographic collection, which had come down in tea chests in a large room on the first floor front, suggesting they keep them close to the walls to relieve the strain on the floor. Halfway through the operation we realised that a 2in gap had appeared between walls and ceiling and every prospect of the priceless collection finishing up on the heads of the mail order department blissfully ignorant below.

We quickly reversed the process and put the collection in the basement thereby continuing the awful life story of these plates. Bombed out of Amen Corner, they had gone to Horseferry Road, the upstairs at Hampton Court then into the basement and later to Shepperton and then to Coombelands before landing up in their final resting place, which we all hope will be the National Railway Museum at York. All the LPC records were in a mess and rather than waste time sorting them out, we had a tremendous bonfire in the garden and got rid of the lot. A practice I often later indulged in much to the chagrin of our various accountants. I worked on the simple premise that if we knew we did not have records no-one would waste time searching through them for something they would probably never find anyway.

'Craven House' had been called 'Wellesley House' and had been the home of the great Duke of Wellington. It was full of character and the rear backed on to Bushy Park. My ground floor office had two balconies over the park and the deer would come up to be friendly; one we nicknamed Elvis, a regular visitor, and adopted as our pet — even Miss Harmer liked him. But Craven House had a few snags: its high ceilinged rooms were always cold and the basement had a very funny smell about it, not surprising really as it was regularly affected by sewage seeping up through the flagstones. It took us a long time to find the cause and we would get one of the chaps from Hampton Court Palace to pop over and rod our manhole which seemed permanently full and was usually released with an almighty slurp, whilst the aforesaid man puffed his cigarette, had a cup of tea and a sandwich but never washed his hands! He loved his good healthy job and said he would not change it for worlds. We loved him too, but never invited him in.

Of course, in those early days of the firm both Mollie and I worked all hours to get things moving and we would both spend hours at weekends cleaning, tidying and generally sprucing up our premises even bringing in anyone we could lay our hands on to help us. Bank managers we found easy prey and I think that few of our early bankers escaped a stint of shop or office refurbishing. Ever since I opened my first account with the princely sum of £40 at the National Provincial Bank on Waterloo station in 1940 I have had nothing but help and co-operation; they were absolutely super — until much later when I had a head-on with them.

But it was not all work and no play, we had a reasonable family and social life as well until one day I was summoned urgently by mother-in-law that Mollie had collapsed whilst shopping with her and she had had to ferry her to her home by taxi. By the time I arrived a doctor had been summoned who obviously could not diagnose the problem; she certainly could not move that evening and I went home to get night things etc and 'phoned our own doctor. In his usual over-optimistic way he telephonically diagnosed the whole matter as stomach ache. By the time I got back to the patient she looked so ill, I thought (rightly) she was at death's door and so obviously did her highly agitated mother who steadfastly refused to have a telephone or use one. I resummoned the doctor who — to his eternal credit — came immediately and quite obviously got the wind up considerably at what he found. Within five minutes he had an ambulance and gave me instructions to follow it, carefully not telling me where it was going.

So mum-in-law and I in an open top 1947 Standard 8 set out from Raynes

*Left:*
**John Cannon with the Flying Standard 8 en route to a visit to the Hastings Miniature Railway.**

*Below:*
**Jim Hughes casts a fatherly eye over 10¼ in *Royal Scot* driven by John Cannon at Hastings. In those early days full-size sleepers provided platform accommodation.**

Park to follow the ambulance into the darkness, for it was nearly midnight. How I kept up I shall never know, we hurtled over tram lines with my little tyres continually skidding in the ruts and my tiny battered old car certainly no match for a powerful bell-ringing ambulance, albeit of 1940s vintage. But we made it and never let the ambulance get out of sight. Eventually we arrived at the Royal Homoeopathic Hospital in Great Ormond Street. Why, Heaven only knows: the ambulance vanished into the bowels of the building and we walked through the front door into a deserted hospital eventually finding a porter who was initially unable to help us; eventually after a prolonged absence he came back and said fairly curtly 'They're opening her up now. No point in waiting, you'd better go home and phone later.'

Somewhat nonplussed I said, 'Yes, let's do just that.' For I never seemed (then or now) to realise the trauma of situations like this. Perhaps I have some inner faith that everything will be all right in the end — as it was in this case. The problem had been an ectopic pregnancy which had caused an internal haemorrhage. My beloved mother-in-law being one of those people who did not discuss things like that had not alerted the doctor to the possibility of something gynaecological, though I am sure she knew that the breeding process was on the agenda. It took us both some time to recover from this ordeal, though I do remember taking a bunch of flowers to the hospital and being giving a lesson on checking the stems of cut flowers to ensure they were fresh unlike the ones I had purchased which were obviously old stock. I haven't bought any flowers since.

Meanwhile back at the ranch an embryonic publishing company was still thriving mainly in the railway 'abc' books. Paper and printing became easier and the long runs 50,000 for the LMS , 40 for the LNER, 30 for the GWR and 25 for the Southern were attractive to suppliers, much sought after by customers and reasonably profitable for us. We had several other winning titles too, *The Locoshed Book*, *Trains Annual*, *Civil Aircraft Markings* and *abc London Transport* to name but a few and our results were generally good. Arthur Baldwin got the sack. Terry Holder took the job of Circulation Manager of the *Economist* and some faint hearts wondered if we could weather the future without them. I (modestly) had no doubt who was running the show and soon recruited replacements. Willie Brett had retired from McCorquodales and deeply involved with the company, offered to come aboard full time and took over in charge of sales and administration. Vic Welch came in from the London Midland Region as artist in place of Arthur Baldwin.

Others too assisted and a new team was created. The first thing Willie did was to bring in one of his mates, Charles Hemmings, as a rep. Charles was a member of the Hemmings' family of South London bakers and had spent his working life selling biscuits. He knew nothing of the book trade and was

51

guilty of the virtually blasphemous comment that if he could sell biscuits, he could sell books or anything else. But he was right. On his first day he came into my office to be formally inducted at exactly 9 o'clock. Hilda Harmer swept in with my morning mail, totally ignoring Charles. As she was about to sweep out I stopped her and said, 'This is Mr Hemmings, our new rep.'

She looked at him disdainfully and snapped, 'Then you'd better get out on the road quickly, you won't sell any books in here' — and I suppose she was quite right. Never let a salesman have a desk or a chair. Charles was as good a salesman as ever Terry Holder was: he was a wisp of a five footer, hard smoking, hard drinking and a hard womaniser, in fact a typical sales-man of the time. Being small he had a slight inferiority complex and was wont to bolster himself up, so when he was given an Austin A30 van to do his calls in, albeit a brand new one, he was unhappy. On the first morning he loaded it up and only got halfway to Kingston before he was pulled up by the police for being overloaded and triumphantly returned to base protesting that he knew the A30 was no good — so he and the Company went fifty fifty on exchanging the A30 for an A90 saloon. This was a very big car for the diminutive Charles who was hardly visible when driving it. Even so he managed to load this until the springs creaked and he did fantastic business with it.

Women buyers were easy prey for Charles and he always secured big orders from them and we asked no questions — though he usually gave the answer quite voluntarily. My first foray with him was to visit customers on the Isle of Wight; I went down by train and arranged to meet him at Ryde. As the ship docked at the pierhead there he was in his A90. I climbed into the passenger seat and he offered me a sweet — 'in the glove box,' he said. As I opened it, a shower of condoms fell out on the floor. I must have made some sort of shocked or feigned shocked comment to which he noncha-lantly replied, 'Don't worry, I'll have used them all by the end of the week.'

In the autumn of 1953 Mollie and I paid a short visit to Brighton. Then in 1954 two things happened. After two weeks of delayed action in June dur-ing the whole of which my car was kept full of petrol and pointing towards the hospital, my wife did manage, successfully, this time, to give birth to our No 1 son, David Ian. The other was noises made by the accountants that we were accumulating profits which must either be invested in the development of the business or distributed or the Inland Revenue would grab them. My sole aim at this stage and after our 1950 financial crisis was to keep a safe balance at the bank to meet all emergencies but apparently that, however acceptable to me and the bank manager, would not be acceptable to the Tax Man. The natural diversification was into printing, so in the basement, albeit smelly, at Craven House, we decided to install a printing unit. We found out the cause of the sewage problem was a broken drain under the A308 Hampton Court Road about 440 yards from Craven House. The cost of digging up this main traffic artery to search for a 150-year old drain was too daunting and we called in Twickenham Council who kindly obliged by sending a sludge gulper which sucked up all our over-flowing cess, blew it at very high pressure down the pipe and after two or three hefty blows and slurps cleared it.

We refurbished the floors, covering the ancient flagstones with watertight composition and installed two Rotaprint machines and the rest of the kit that went with them. Our caretaker who had come to us as a packer at London Bridge and lived on the second floor, agreed to train as a Rotaprint operator and quickly began turning out excellent work. He in turn appointed a young female assistant, a quiet but very attractive girl. Obviously he was ribbed as to what they got up to in the basement which he always strongly denied on the basis that as his wife lived on the premises he could not possibly do anything amiss. He was overtly a quiet South London boy, always deferential and polite though we had the feeling that duly motivated he could be fairly 'wide'. Indeed he had been suspected of some disappearing blank red postal orders until Miss Harmer had saved him by nailing the real culprit. One day Jim, the caretaker, and I wanted to get into the building and neither of us had the key. 'No problem,' he said and literally ran up the side of the house, flicked a window catch on the first floor and in a jiffy was in and I wondered how many other houses he had entered like that in his time.

One day he appeared in the office black and blue from head to foot, with a swollen face, closed-up eyes and two broken ribs. He had had, he said, an altercation in Molesey and been thrown bodily through a shop window. The reason for his beating up was never divulged and he recovered after a few weeks. Then suddenly he despatched his heavily pregnant wife and two small sons to her family in Newcastle for a visit. She went off and very soon afterwards so did he — in the opposite direction and his attractive printing side kick disappeared too. Nothing was ever heard of either of them again.

Stranded in the north his poor wife gave birth and with nowhere to live was given temporary shelter by a farmer. One of our staff who had been friendly with her and kept in touch by correspondence, visited her and found the baby bedded in a drawer and the two boys running wild. On her return she told me of the family's plight and we sent them some money and some sympathy. Two days later she was on the office door step complete with three children. I now realise we did the worst possible thing, though with the best possible motive, we took her out of the 'system'. We should have taken the family straight to Twickenham Council and let the community service department take over but in those days things were not as sophisti-

*Above:*
**The flag that caused all the trouble at Craven House, Hampton Court.**

*Right:*
**A 1955 photograph of the vehicle fleet outside Craven House with attendant staff, obviously waiting for something to happen. The flag staff and name plate, which offended the council so much, can be seen.**

54

cated as they are now and in desperation to get them accommodated, we acquired for them a caravan on a site in Chertsey. At least they had shelter and a reasonable environment and facilities. Within days the brand new caravan was being wrecked, one of the boys was in trouble with the police and obviously the whole family was unable to cope. Fortunately the Council stepped in, and we donated the caravan which was sold to help set them up in proper accommodation. We never heard another word from any of them.

Thus I learnt the salutary lesson that some staff — not all by any means but quite a lot — will take you for a very long ride and however much you try to help will in the end not even give you a 'thank you' for your trouble.

Anyway, after all that little saga we had a printing company and called it Ian Allan Printing Ltd. We now had four companies, the original Ian Allan Ltd, Ian Allan Printing Ltd and the two we had acquired, Loco Pub Co Ltd and Railway Publications Ltd, the brain child of one of our blockmakers who had produced a railway quiz book, intended to be the forerunner of many more, but which was, in fact, a rather damp squib in which he quickly became disinterested.

Life at Craven House was not all beer and skittles. We had a running battle with Twickenham Borough Council whose planning committee, I suspect, resented the fact that we had won an appeal against their refusal to allow us to use the building for business purposes. In 1952 we tidied up the front of the premises and erected a flag staff from which we flew a flag with our name on it. This immediately provoked a reaction — take it down. In order

to pour oil on the troubled waters, we agreed to apply officially for planning permission to fly a 'trade flag' assuming that any other flag would be OK. To our amazement the application came quickly back with the comment that as we did not have planning consent for the flag staff itself, consideration could not be given to flying a flag from it. This rather got up my nose and I wrote and told the Council in no uncertain terms, concurrently sending the story out to the press and pointing out that it would have been nice to fly our Union Jack during Coronation year. The press picked it up wonderfully — half a page in the *Daily Express*, a large lump in the *Telegraph* each with pictures. Within two days, a letter came from Twickenham's Town Clerk replying to my forthright epistle, 'Whilst it is not the Council's policy to respond to letters couched in offensive terms' ... they had reconsidered and we were free to fly our flag.

We had made our point and on the next fracas provoked by the Borough Engineer, the Town Clerk, Chairman of the Planning Committee and others asked if they could call to sort out the problem. We had a happy tea party together and we all lived happily ever after.

One useful friend I had made during my sojourn on the Southern Railway was with the refreshment department at Waterloo which not only ran all the station catering facilities but the restaurant cars as well. Every year we would hold a trade dinner for our customers in the first floor restaurant which was closed to the public in the evenings, but more enjoyable were our staff outings. There were only about 30 of us in those days and the Southern would attach an extra restaurant car direct to the rear of the 0830 to Weymouth, stop it specially at Surbiton and feed us for the day at either Swanage or Lymington as we chose; the restaurant car being detached and attached at Wareham or Brockenhurst respectively. They always did us proud but the catering was expensive, or seemed so then; the five course lunch was 12s 6d and the seven course dinner was 19s 6d. What super trips they were and the refreshment manager and his wife even did the catering for our firstborn's christening party.

# 5
# Hampton Court

We were now publishing books on any form of transport, merchant ships had taken us into warships, lorries had taken us into military vehicles and so our range covered militaria fairly substantially. In an unguarded moment, I had in the early 1950s succumbed to an approach from Sidney Prichard who wanted to buy *Railway Modeller* which we had started from our association with Allan Brett Cannon. He offered £200 for it but was so hard up he said he would have to pay in two instalments. We were so hard up and *Railway Modeller* was losing us money that we accepted. Mr Peco got the bargain of a lifetime and did jolly well with it for which he deserves personal congratulations. Cyril Freezer who had been our editor moved with the magazine to Seaton and the success they all made of it is well known. You can't win 'em all and I have learnt long ago never to job backwards, one makes what seems to be the right decision at the time and makes the best of it thereafter.

So when W. J. Fowler made noises that they would like to sell us *Railway World* and *Model Railway Constructor*, we seized the opportunity to get back into the model railway market and accepted *Railway World* as something of an incubus. It had a circulation of about 8,000 and was in the same market as *Trains Illustrated*. We did the deal and bought Railway World Ltd, its two magazines and stock. The stories related by the editor, Ken Mansell, who came with the deal, were legion; old man Fowler was a republican through and through and is reputed to have had a notice in his office, 'This is the Republic of Tramway' and his dislike of the monarchy was matched only by his hatred of buses which had replaced his beloved trams. The day after the King died in 1952 Mansell recalled a note on his desk, 'No mention of George'. Mystified, he sought enlightenment from the old man who spelled it out that no reference to the King's death, or, indeed, life, should be made in *Railway World*. As editor, Mansell objected and insisted that some mark of respect had to be included and there was compromise — Mansell inserted his tribute and *one* personal copy of the magazine was printed for the Chairman without the reference.

Thus we had quite a clutch of magazines and bred a company unusual in the publishing world which produced both books and magazines. This is a mixture which does not blend comfortably and which was perhaps the bane

*Above:*
**London steam in the 1950s with a train of ancient stock in East London.**

*Below:*
**The 'Potteries Express', headed by No 42922, joins the Macclesfield line at North Rode on 9 May 1959.**

of our life in later years. The advantage, of course, was regular and totally free contact with the reading public and cost free advertising and promotion. Promotion which led to the operation of all those special trains on British Railways, who always co-operated superbly; the punters loved them, and most of our customers were children and in those days BR was not run by accountants and did not realise how much money they must have lost in those marvellous excursions. But money was/is not everything. The great pool of goodwill BR built up in those days has spilled into the great pool of friends who support BR today against the barrage of criticism. The railway enthusiast is a far better PRO than ever the myriad chaps who bear the title and collect the spondulix from it. As Grasemann once said to me, a PRO's job is to keep things out of the papers more than to get them in. And I here interject a little tale, one of Grasemann's sorties into direct PR. At a civic lunch at Littlehampton to mark the electrification of the line in the 1930s he is alleged to have concluded his post-prandial speech, 'Now Littlehampton's greatest amenity is the excellent train service by which you can get away from it,' which did not go down too well.

Notwithstanding after our 1953 trip, we paid another visit to Brighton in the autumn of 1956 and lo and behold, Son No 2 arrived by Caesarian section in August 1957. My wife by now had decided that she and child bearing were not entirely compatible so we shut up the shutters on further family expansion and left it for the two boys to do this in later years (which they did very successfully) and we steamed out of the 1950s with a financially strong company, a firm base at Hampton Court and a somewhat enlarged family, with a firm resolve not to stay in Brighton again.

I have always believed that serendipity has played a major part in my life and things have happened without really any input from me. In 1955 my Uncle Harry asked me suddenly whether I would like to join the freemasons, remarking that my father had been in the chair of his Lodge when he died and how well they had got on together when they both came into the Craft. I declined in the certain knowledge that with a young family starting, my absence at Lodge meetings would not go down too well with materfamilias. Uncle Harry was persuasive, invited me to sign the application form in the certain knowledge that there was a long waiting list and that it would be yonx before I got in. I duly signed the form, appeared before the committee, confessed that my wife did not approve and thought I had sunk back into oblivion. That was not to be for as a 'lewis' or son of a mason, I took priority over everyone else and was up for initiation almost immediately. In for a penny, in for a pound, I went 'through' and subsequently progressed through the various offices and never for a moment regretted Uncle Harry's persuasive powers. I have thoroughly enjoyed my masonic experiences of which even the aforementioned *'er indoors* now thoroughly

*Above:*
**Double-headed by tank engines the train leaves Macclesfield. Note the Pullman observation car running as second coach; this is currently on the Paignton & Dartmouth Railway.**

approves. My initiation in 1955 had a resounding effect on the Company later on — in 1972 to be precise but more of that later.

One of our neighbours, Bryan Corrie, a solicitor who acted for us from time to time, paid a visit to Craven House way back in 1960 and as he left the building, as a throw-away line he said, 'How much longer are you going to stay here? Isn't it time you moved on?' It set me thinking and fortuitously too as will be seen, and I began to get itchy feet: after all Craven House was old, cold, inconvenient, frequently smelly, so who to turn to but dear old BR. I wrote to the Estate Department at Victoria and very tentatively asked if they had any spare land in the vicinity suitable for building a small office block. To my surprise and delight, there came back a quick response and a suggestion that land at Shepperton might be available: this was great news, an office only two miles from home within easy cycling, even walking distance. But there was to be many a slip twixt cup and lip and the ultimate impasse only unblocked by the intervention of the Chairman of the British Transport Commission himself. The necessity to move suddenly became urgent. The Inspector of Taxes was not content with our just developing a printing company. He wanted to attack the rest of our undistributed resources: after some argument he accepted our contention that we needed them to pay for our new offices and gave us one year to start work — or else.

Shepperton station in 1961 consisted of two lines with an engine release crossover at the country end and two platforms, the up one being totally isolated and never used. On either side were strips of land used for allotments and a vast and elaborate Southern Railway advertising hoarding surrounding the buffer stops. The estate people offered the strip on the down side at a ground rent of £1,000 a year for a 42-year lease which all sounded reasonable and plans were drawn up. They were immediately rejected by the local authority on the basis that a building line had to be complied with so the 30ft wide planned building had to be slimmed to 20ft which at once reduced the floor space by a third. Back then to BR who agreed to lease the north side of the railway for a similar period and charge. So the ground rent doubled overnight as did the cost of building two establishments instead of one.

Back to Sunbury Council who were unhappy about the whole project and wondered why on earth we could not settle somewhere else — anywhere else — and said so in as many words. The chaps from Middlesex County Council, however, came to our rescue and with some knowledge of our rough and tumbles with Twickenham Council turned a sympathetic ear and eventually planning consent was granted for the two buildings linked by a bridge across the railway. Out to tender we went, at the same time as negotiating the legalities of the lease. We selected the tender from Gazes of Kingston and fixed a starting date subject to the formal lease documents from BR. After nearly two years of negotiation, BR suddenly slapped on the brakes. Someone in the operating department at Waterloo had decided that as they were considering 10-car trains on the South Western division, it might be necessary to extend the platform and thereby scupper our development plan. With builders waiting to go, and the whole operation geared up, the prospect of either abandoning or going back to the drawing board with all its architectural, planning and building regulation complications was more than flesh and blood could stand. Having failed to register the point with the Estate Department who merely stood back and bowed to the Operators, I fired a salvo off to Sir Brian Robertson, Chairman of the British

Transport Commission. To my surprise and delight, within a couple of days the problem was over, the lease arrived and building commenced.

One great objective I had was to build in and preserve an interesting vehicle in our complex. Frank Harding of the Pullman Car Co readily agreed to a request to purchase a suitable vehicle and selected *Malaga* for us. This was a 1922 wooden bodied 1st class kitchen car which had been refurbished in 1949 for service on the 'Golden Arrow' but more especially for use by the King and his journeys on the Southern. The vehicle has six-wheel bogies and special walnut veneered aluminium based panelling and unique hand-tooled copper designs depicting the various goodies available from Pullman cars — a sheep, depicting meat, fish, grapes and corn. Harding had the vehicle completely repainted at the Pullman works at Brighton and a boardroom table built inside the main saloon. One Sunday it duly arrived at Shepperton complete with a 45-ton crane, a brake van and steam locomotive, a rare sight indeed for Shepperton. With loving care the foreman supervised the fixing of the chains round the body and at 11.45 said, 'Now for it, let's hope it doesn't break its back.' The lift started and there was an

*Above:*
**Lonely *Malaga* arrives on site at Shepperton.**

horrendous creak, but no problem, the coach body was thus suspended across both tracks with the bogies still on the running line. '12 o'clock, the pub's open,' he said and the whole team streamed into the nearby 'Crossroads Inn' where Guinness was liberally quaffed.

At 13.45 I decided to leave the party to get my lunch and was amazed to hear that the team's ETD was 15.00 in view of the fact that apart from lifting the body, nothing further had been done. I made a small wager with them that they would still be there when I returned after 3pm. I lost. On my return at 15.15 *Malaga* was happily sitting on its own little bit of track, securely 'scotched' and resplendent on its bogies. I was delighted.

The arrival of *Malaga* was the third phase determining the commencement of construction work on Terminal House, the other two being the planners and the BR lease. Work began in earnest, perhaps we were too fussy, perhaps the architect could have done a better supervising job, perhaps the builders were a bit sloppy — anyway the following six months were somewhat fraught with ourselves, our architect and our builders most of the time at each other's throats. But we were proud of our new building albeit not a particularly beautiful structure but one designed and built subject to the confined area available and the 42-year lease, for as the building would then revert to the landlord, it seemed prudent that the building's life and that of the lease should be co-terminal. Another mistaken idea, for BR's policy on land sales vacillated and from refusing to sell freeholds they suddenly offered us ours which we grabbed but wished we had built a better building.

When I say we had a few ups and downs with builders, I suppose I am putting it mildly. One epic was the cross-railway bridge connecting our two buildings: according to the plans this was positioned at right angles on both sides reached by a short flight of stairs to a small landing in either building. The bridge was prefabricated and delivered on site and was to be put in position by BR steam crane which came down especially in the middle of Saturday/Sunday night. Next morning when I went to view the building, the bridge was up. BR had done its stuff, the juice was back on and the crane and loco departed. But ugh! We had a skew bridge and, indeed, have one to this day: architect and builder tried to convince me that all was according to plan and nearly succeeded until I suddenly rumbled that someone had failed to realise that the ground levels of the two buildings were not the same so that had they used the originally designed resting places we should have a sloping bridge and so the experts had opted for the easier choice of slewing it. I was furious and the whole story eventually tumbled out that there in the middle of the night with a bridge dangling from a BR crane and anxious to return to base, the professionals had to solve a big problem and hope nobody noticed the fundamental error.

*Above:*
**Before — the crossroads at Shepperton in December 1963.**

*Below:*
**After — the same scene in November 1965.**

The builders then used the wrong sort of plaster on the walls which did not adhere properly and has been breaking away for the last 30 years; doorways appeared where they should not and did not appear where they should but eventually it was complete. BR had insisted that the bridge was made in such a way that they could dismantle parts to inspect it every two years. It has now stood for 30 and no inspector has ever been near it.

Charles Klapper, that doyen of the transport world and editor of *Modern Transport*, who had slated me so vociferously in the Aldwych Brasserie in 1944, invited me to an expensive lunch with his chairman at the Hunting Lodge in Piccadilly: they were in financial problems and wanted to be bought out. *Modern Transport* with its self ascribed soubriquet 'The Times of the Transport World', was a highly prestigious weekly newspaper and the prospect of taking it on board as an Ian Allan publication was mouth watering as, indeed, was *Passenger Transport* offered some weeks previously by the *News of the World* organisation. *Passenger Transport* was easy to assimilate as a one-man job. *Modern Transport* was a different kettle of fish but we took it on at a fairly knock-down price, though I realised to my horror that in the end by taking over the company I had paid for that expensive lunch at the Hunting Lodge, complete with premises in Woburn Place. It brought with it Charles Klapper, John Burman, John Parke, Bill Cornwell plus three or four others. Advertising revenue was hard to come by and circulation remained impossible to shift and we had to shed some staff though Klapper, Cornwell and Parke stayed to the end of their working lives. *Modern Transport*, having failed to wash its financial face and having proved to me that everything I touched did not necessarily turn to gold, was gently laid to rest. *Passenger Transport* was combined with *Buses* and has remained so ever since.

The *Modern Transport* gang were the first to move into Terminal House and before the plumbing was established; fortunately nearby Shepperton station was available for physical needs and there was a steady flow (sic) from Terminal House until the builders had screwed up the last pipe. We moved our bank account from the National Westminster at Kingston to the Shepperton branch where the local manager Bob Rowland was the virtual godfather of the village. We moved the firm on a Saturday, and the Bank really came up trumps, most of the staff came over and helped unload the lorries of furniture and more importantly book stock, which was heavy and bulky. Their co-operation was magnificent but there was one serious misjudgement. I had fondly imagined that we would close the office in Hampton Court on Friday and everyone would be happily working at Shepperton on Monday. Human nature is not like that, nearly all the Hampton Court staff disliked the move; their lunch-time 2d bus ride to Kingston, to Bentalls and all the other shops was sorely missed and Shepperton's then handful of village shops did not bear comparison. Miss Harmer complained that it was bad enough getting from Selhurst to Hampton Court and Shepperton was even worse. Nevertheless, she coped well and was usually still first to arrive and last to leave. However, we slowly but surely turned over nearly all the staff, recruiting new members from the local area.

The architect had designed a large reception area in the new offices in which it was planned to build a large show model railway. But when the time came, it would obviously be a waste of some very valuable space and whilst we were thinking what to do about it all, Alan Pegler (who probably needs no introduction and whom I had known for years as a rabid enthusiast and subsequently owner of 4472 *Flying Scotsman*) rang to say that Trevor Bailey, one of his co-directors on the newly resuscitated Festiniog Railway, was looking for something to do as the family had recently sold its surgical instrument business. Trevor then phoned me and said he was thinking of going into Travel, an idea which Geoffrey Allen had also strongly advised that we should move into. 'Do you know anything about Travel?' we both asked each other and on receiving negative assurances, decided it was an excellent starting point. The company would supply a shop (ie, large reception area, intended to be a model railway) a telephone and a desk; Trevor would acquire the know-how. Of course, we already had a formidable business based on our special trains for railway enthusiasts and these formed a good base for the new enterprise.

Trevor was terrific: a great personality and totally charming. It took a great deal to ruffle his feathers and he quickly built up a thriving retail travel business in tiny Shepperton, something which took us all by surprise. The travel industry was in its infancy and we were in on the ground floor, with the world our oyster. It cost very little to set up a travel shop as no stock was involved; you found the shop, selected the manager and virtually opened the front door. It got progressively more difficult as the trade became more sophisticated. ABTA crept in and IATA was jealous of its licences so that a new professionalism had to develop. We began to race ahead, opening a branch at nearby Ashford and over the years by various means another 32 branches until we had a turnover of some £40 million a year. Little did we think that from that brief phone call from Alan Pegler such a business would develop or that from our proposed model railway exhibition/reception space a considerable empire would rise.

# 6

# Moving to Shepperton

We were now assembling quite a range of companies: Ian Allan Ltd, the original publishing company; Ian Allan Locospotters' Club Ltd; Ian Allan Developments Ltd into which we poured our property resources plus the others we had been picking up and our advisers recommended that all should be tidied up with a Group. We, therefore, formed Ian Allan Group Ltd in 1962 with most of its shares held in a family trust and this company in turn became the proprietor of all the other companies who were, of course, now 'fellow subsidiary companies'. Apart from the small shareholding of Cecil J. Allen, which was inherited by Geoffrey Allen and ultimately passed to Norman Miles who became our finance director in 1971 until he retired in 1990 when it returned to the family, there have never been any outside shareholders.

It took a long time to settle in Shepperton, the purpose-built premises gave us plenty of space but things got a bit tough and in 1965 a great blow hit us. Steam locomotives were to be withdrawn from BR and Beeching was in full swing: this would seem to be going to do us no good at all and I became depressed at the prospect of being a railway publisher with very little railway to publish about. Of course, I — as usual — over-reacted, steam took some years to go and the great nostalgia interest started to grow. In fact, books on railways became in far greater demand than even before. Then suddenly onto the scene appeared a chap from the British Printing Corporation; this was a growing conglomerate built up by take-over after take-over, including Waterlows, Rymans and other household names from the Somerset-based printers Purnells at Paulton headed by Wilfred Harvey. They were out for a take-over and after a few preliminary discussions with the side kick, a friendly enough chap and co-director of Harvey, whom I suspected of looking for a backhander for himself, the great man himself came to Shepperton arriving tactlessly at the front door in an enormous Rolls-Royce.

Harvey far from being 'great' was a small, friendly and most amiable West Countryman who called everyone 'm'dear' and had a manner which really induced you to walk into his parlour. He invited me to Paulton and presided over a regular lunch party with his senior colleagues personally carving the joint and serving each one of us individually. He made me very

H STREET, SHEPPERTON-ON-THAMES. 4291

WEIR, SHEPPERTON-ON-THAMES

**Shepperton became the Company's home in the 1960s and, nearly 30 years later we're still here. These pictures show the older end nearer the Thames.**

*Above left:*
**The War Memorial and bottom of the High Street.**

*Below left:*
**Shepperton Weir.**

*Right:*
**St Nicholas' Church.**

*Below:*
**Shepperton Lock.**

ST. NICHOLAS CHURCH, SHEPPERTON-ON-THAMES          4289

SHEPPERTON-ON-THAMES

69

welcome and I almost felt a member of his management team there and then. The advent of the Rolls-Royce at Terminal House had set tongues wagging and everyone wondered what was in the air and eventually we struck a deal whereby BPC bought 91% of our shares with the option to purchase the balance at a later date. But then suddenly it was *Harvey* who was going to purchase the shares — not BPC as originally negotiated — and we wondered why and suspected that Harvey having obtained our shares would sell them on to BPC at an enhanced price. But it did not happen. At the last minute neither Harvey nor BPC could raise the cash and could only offer BPC shares instead. Fortunately we had the sense to refuse and withdrew from the deal and we remained independent.

Shortly afterwards Harvey and some of his colleagues went up for trial on various fraud charges and this interesting little chapter in our lives closed. BPC later went into the Robert Maxwell empire and we all know what happened to him, though his demise reminded me of our early days of publishing when one of our main customers was the firm of Simpkin Marshall Ltd, one of the few national book wholesalers in the country. They were a sleepy old firm but did good business though probably not very profitably: suddenly a new wind blew into publishing in the shape of Robert Maxwell who acquired Simpkin Marshall and started to build up its throughput. We were delighted with the extra orders until suddenly, bang, it went bust. Maxwell walked away with or without some of its assets and left the publishing trade some very large bad debts, in our case £1,500 which was big money for a small firm in the late 1940s. Something I had never forgotten and which amazed me when I later saw him swashbuckling on his luxury yacht and often thought of writing to suggest he repaid the £1,500 with interest.

Talking about crooks, during our time we have encountered all sorts of thieving and frauds which are never very pleasant especially when one implements the avowed company policy of reporting all cases to the Police and supporting the actions they take thereafter. We had one manager of a Travel shop who helped himself to £500 out of the till at the same time as he was putting himself up for the local Council — our Council. When I told him I expected him to withdraw his nomination he looked aghast and asked, 'Why?' Even when the reason was spelled out to him he still could not understand our extraordinary attitude until I suggested we advised the local Conservative office of his exploits when he changed his mind.

The more extraordinary case was that of a police sergeant at Hampton who happened one Saturday afternoon to be walking through Teddington when for some reason he went into a bookshop and announced himself as Sergeant Bloggs. The proprietor is alleged to have blurted out, 'Thank goodness you've come, I can't stand the worry any more,' or words to that effect. The sergeant was led to an Aladdin's cave at the back of the shop containing what appeared to be a large slab of our warehouse stock. Further investigation disclosed a network of intrigue involving packers, reps and van drivers.

Our system at the time was that to release a consignment on invoice set consisting of delivery note, numbered label and invoice went into the packing department. Proof of dispatch and security was provided by the numbered label which was logged with the weight of the parcel and the destination details. Our clever chaps had evolved a system where they packed one load with invoice and affixed a separate label with the magic number on and then packed a duplicate consignment using the original numbered label and delivery note. It seemed that it was a split consignment but, of course, actually it was a duplicate. All the van driver had to do was to deliver one parcel and flog the contents of the other and put the cash in the syndicate. The other stunt was to take an order addressed to a provincial customer, say W. H. Smith of Sheffield, and do the same duplication trick but marking parcels, 'To be called for at Sheffield station'. The local rep was then advised and he would collect both parcels, deliver one and flog the contents of the other.

*Above:*
**The completed Terminal House in 1964 showing the Midland Railway distant signal gracing the front garden and the original Shepperton station building in the background.**

The sergeant's fortuitous visit to Teddington caused the sacking and prosecution of several trusted staff and for all the police trouble and vast loss of thousands of pounds' worth of stock, the perpetrators got a derisory six months' suspended sentence.

Less fortunate was a director of our Motor Company who also tried his luck at getting his own private cars repaired on the basis of false insurance claims that they were entirely different company cars. He got six months' inside as did one of our car salesmen who managed to sell our cars for cash and get the money mixed up with his own.

I have always found it very hard to decide to shop people who are obviously guilty of serious breaches on the basis of 'there but for the grace of God go I'. Alas, one has to be tough or the discipline of the company would fall apart and the genuinely honest majority would give up. And one can so easily find oneself inadvertently on the wrong side of the law and facing dire penalties — as we go on the risk gets greater. We fell into a pothole under the Restrictive Practices Act where an apparently innocent sales agreement with W. H. Smith was deemed restrictive. We remained under threat of prosecution for several years and when the case eventually came up the Judge threw it out on the basis of unreasonable delay and awarded us over £20,000 in costs. Less lucky are you, however, when you fall foul of the myriad rules and regulations of Inland Revenue, DHSS and Customs & Excise and even our army of Chartered Accountants have failed to put their fingers in every hole.

Bryan Corrie caused me to be invited to join the Rotary Club of Shepperton; in itself a not very remarkable achievement but I enjoyed membership and the relationship it gave me with the nobility and gentry of Shepperton, at that time still a small business community mostly of principals. It was later to prove a fundamental cog in the development of Ian Allan Group as had been the case of my advent into masonry 10 years earlier. In those days every rotarian represented a different profession in business; there were Corrie the Solicitor, Channon the Estate Agent (both our next door neighbours at Terminal House) Fisher the Architect to name but a few. They came into our business and general life and once we had got over the initial shock of our move from Hampton Court, we realised that it was the best move we ever made or could have made.

# 7

# Miniature Railways

Alastair MacLeod, my old friend from Waterloo, retired as Chief Stores Superintendent LM Region Euston and came down the line from his home station at Wimbledon on a fairly regular basis and ultimately 'adopted' us. He did not think much of the disorderly way we kept our reference library and vast collection of pictures and set about to put it right. What a splendid job he made of it with his meticulous care and attention to detail. It was not long before he was coming in every day in exchange for a free lunch in our captive Pullman car *Malaga* where very high fallutin' and technical conversation between him, Charles Klapper and Basil Cooper, a well known railway writer and at the time working on *Railway World*, soon had everyone else buying sandwiches in the pub rather than face an hour or even half an hour as a passive audience listening to the merits and demerits of the enlarged bunkers on 02 Class locomotives or the number of rivets in a 'King's' tender. MacLeod soon became 'Uncle Mac' and continued a close association almost to the day he died in 1990.

Mac knew of my interest in miniature railways, indeed, he and I had frequently driven together on the RH&DR and Hastings Miniature Railway, still thriving under the management of Jim Hughes: he invited me over to the Walton home of the late Sir John Samuel who had recently died to show me the mysteries of the Greywood Central Railway. This was a fascinating 7¼in gauge line which went in and out and roundabout the acre garden behind the Samuel home on the Burwood Park estate. The point of my visit soon became apparent. 'Pinkie' Samuel, John's widow, had decided to sell the house and did not know what to do about the railway. 'Could you,' asked Mac, 'find a home for it?' I demurred.

With the successive deaths of the various partners in the Hastings Miniature Railway set-up, the ownership was now vested jointly in myself, Willie Brett and John Cannon. This unholy trinity had in the early 1960s bought speculatively a farm and 56 acres near Chertsey and having sold off the buildings had a residual 56 acres of land — an ideal home for the Greywood Central Railway; the leading lights headed by Mac came to view it, deemed it suitable and to the land owners' united amazement a week later they found a complete railway literally dumped on their land. I was apprehensive, Willie Brett was furious and John Cannon enthusiastic. We eventually sorted out

*Above:*
**Class 'K4' 2-6-0 No 3442 *The Great Marquess* pilots Class 'A3' No 4472 *Flying Scotsman* on the Ian Allan special from King's Cross and Leeds City to Darlington. They are seen shortly after leaving Harrogate on 3 October 1964.**

*Below:*
**The original *Thunderbolt* with a train of ex-Hilton Valley railway coaches redesignated GCR.**

our own problem by which time enthusiastic mini-railwaymen were digging out trenches without so much as a by your leave from the owners who were none too pleased. Shortly after Mac arrived in the office complete with a Southern Railway shorthand notebook in which was a complete inventory of the rails, points, rolling stock, locomotives and to my amazement, evaluated in detail. It took me a little while to rumble what he was on about as his approach was uncharacteristically far from direct until he finished up, 'So if you will let me have your cheque, I will give it to Lady Samuel.' It was never the idea that any purchase was involved as all that had originally been suggested was the 'finding' of a home. However, there it was and as I find it hard to part unexpectedly (or even expectedly) with money, I asked for more time to consider. In the end the deal looked fair enough and Ian Allan (Miniature Railway Supplies) Ltd was conceived for this acquisition sparked off the possibility of providing equipment for commercial miniature railways nationwide.

Foremost amongst the ex-Greywood brigade were Phillip Simpson, a very tetchy solicitor from the Church Commissioners, Chris Bishop a confectionery wholesaler, and Dennis Baglow, a light engineer from Byfleet. Dennis and Phillip surveyed the route and months elapsed while drains were dug and levels established: all far too slow for my liking; I wanted to get my newly acquired *Eureka*, a hybrid GCR 'Pacific' on the move. But this was not to be for some time and I got very edgy at the lack of immediate results so turned to other things. We heard that Bognor Regis was looking for a miniature railway and rallied the support of a local engineer, Rotarian Alf Pitfield, who with MacLeod designed a fairly simple 0-4-0 diesel locomotive (obviously named the *Pitfield Thunderbolt*) bought three coaches from the Hilton Valley Railway and opened our first sea-side railway at Bognor. The coaches were far too heavy and cumbersome and wont to derail; the loco's wheelbase was too long and too rigid and its steel wheels soon had the circular aluminium track in shreds. We learnt a lot from this little episode which was, in fact, quite profitable and went on to better things, this time in 10¼in gauge. Mac designed a bigger locomotive but with a distinct family likeness to his 'Thunderbolt' class and designated it 'Meteor'. Alf Pitfield then went into production on building 'Meteors' and we had established railways at Whitby, Bournemouth, Sandown, Prestatyn, Buxton, Bognor (2) as well as the existing line at Hastings which had now come under the IA(MRS) umbrella.

Phillip Simpson retired, became much less tetchy, even lovably amicable, and he and John Cannon masterminded the negotiation, construction, layout and operation of a quite complex system all over the country. It all seemed fine to me but John and Phillip took the brunt of what happened next. There were late night calls from corporate entertainment managers of technical problems which necessitated the team taking off at short notice to

*Above:*
**10¼ in gauge miniature railway in Hotham Park, Bognor Regis.**

*Below:*
**The miniature railway was popular at Prestatyn, though the sand played havoc with the mechanics when the wind got up.**

*Above:*
**At Stapleford Park, Ian Allan inspects the merits of the Curwen 'Atlantic' which he drove on many occasions, watched by the late Lord Gretton and his son John who succeeded to the title but sadly died some years ago.**

put things right. Phillip Simpson had been a racing driver and practised his powers in racing all over the country with either John or me as somewhat unwilling passengers. When he could be persuaded to take a rest and let one of us drive, he would exhort us on continually with, 'Take him, take him,' when we came across a car ahead and if he would not move fast enough, 'Singe the back of his neck with your head lights!'

But I digress. Back at Chertsey the new Greywood line was taking shape: the nearby Cockcrow Hill conveniently lent its name to the new operation and Greywood Central Railway became Great Cockcrow Railway thereby maintaining the initials GCR and the overtones of the Great Central Railway which had obviously been John Samuel's pet.

But officialdom was to strike. Chertsey Council began to make noises about planning consents being required. We argued that none had been required at Walton and on the basis that if we applied and were turned down, we had a negative situation; if we did not apply we could not be refused, so we

*Above:*
**The new generation of engine driving Allans;**
**11-year old Paul has his first driving lesson on the 7¼in Great Cockcrow Railway.**

refused to apply QED. John Cannon, however, lived in Chertsey and was fairly well-known and did not like the idea of flying in the face of the Council and cajoled me to go and talk to the Council's Engineer who he assured me would be amenable. He certainly was, all he wanted was a footplate ride on a mainline locomotive and this I duly arranged: he went down to Salisbury on a 'King Arthur' and came back so chuffed he was quite prepared to forget all about his planning problem. Later we had just got to the end of a second interview at which he was about to confirm that we could go ahead regardless when he had second thoughts and felt he should call in his planning officer. This gent was entirely antipathetic, a typical local government bureaucrat who threw up every objection to going ahead without all the necessary consents. Eventually after much lobbying — not by us — we were virtually guaranteed that if we applied officially for planning consent it would be granted. Chertsey were as good as their word, we played ball and so did they and just like Twickenham we all lived happily together ever after even later being officially recognised by Surrey County Council as a tourist attraction and included in the official guide.

For the first five years I was never really accepted as part of the railway any more than was John Cannon and as we both virtually owned the show we did get a little vexed at times but hope we did not show it — much — though we did have an up and downer from time to time with some of the lads who having donned pseudo railway clothes suddenly became dominatingly aggressive — a sight seen later on so many preserved railways enacting the behaviour of some of their prototypical colleagues.

Eventually the railway was complete or rather Phase 1 was. It had an embryonic signalling system and we started to enjoy it. To make sure we had no further problem with the local authority, the Chairman of the Council was invited to open the railway and duly turned up with his lady in their best bibs and tuckers and chains of office. There had been torrential rain in the morning but the sun shone for the ceremonial. The Chairman cut the tape and was conveyed on the first train. On his return he looked rather enviously at *Thunderbolt* and I asked him whether he would like a drive, an invitation he readily accepted. After a short lesson, he, madam and others departed in the civic train. Alas, it did not return, and 30 minutes later a mud-smeared Councillor and his lady staggered back to the station: the morning's deluge had taken its toll of the new earthworks and the heavy *Thunderbolt* was too much for them, they collapsed as did all the stout parties who finished up unceremoniously in a very muddy ditch.

From those early days a magnificent railway has emerged. Unashamedly we claim it to be the finest 7¼in gauge railway in the world, staffed entirely by volunteers with an age span of 9 to 82 and from every walk of life including quite a few full time senior railwaymen.

# 8

# Alarums and Excursions

The development of excursions for locospotters has already been mentioned but as time went on our trips became more sophisticated and we were selecting our own engines and rolling stock and finding routes over which to run them which could not be encompassed by ordinary service trains. One 'best effort' was to run a 'Castle' up the Lickey incline, the plan for which met some resistance at first but we had a super contact with BR, Dennis Williams, who as long as anything started on the Western Region, seemed to be able in his very quiet way to pull every string in the book. He came into the office one day and said he could give no information on this trip as clearance tests had to be carried out with the 'Castle' and these could not take place for at least a month. Such, however, was our network of spies on BR that I was able to produce a photograph taken a week earlier of the aforesaid 'Castle' actually traversing the Lickey. 'Oh,' said the indefatigable Dennis, 'You seem to be better informed than I am.' He could have said that again for the editorial department of Ian Allan Ltd is *always* better informed than BR's official spokespersons.

Trevor Bailey came to me one day in 1963 and asked if I realised that 9 May 1964 was the 60th anniversary of *City of Truro's* record breaking 100mph on Wellington Bank. He suggested that we tried to persuade BR to hit 100mph again, certainly the first attempt since the war. Persuaded no doubt by Dennis Williams, BR agreed. Two 'Castles', *Pendennis* and *Clun*, were to be used and the run would be non-stop to Plymouth and back calling only at Bristol on the return journey. Stand-by engines were positioned at Taunton facing west in the morning and turned to face east in the afternoon and also at Swindon.

Locomotive Inspector Bill Andress was to be in charge in the down direction and Jack Hancock would take over at Bristol for the return when it was planned to do the 100mph on the flat between there and Didcot. Bill Andress was upset that he was not to preside over the 100mph attempt but quietly confided to me and Trevor that he intended to do it with *Pendennis* on the down run. Bill Thorley, who was motive power boss for the WR at the time, was on the train riding with me and in charge of the train was WR's Chief Inspector Richards, resplendent in gold braid and every inch a Great Western man.

*Above:*
**An early locospotters' excursion by diesel railcar with a group from Newbury. On the extreme right is O. J. Morris and in front of him BR's indefatigable Dennis Williams.**

*Below:*
**On 9 May 1964 Ian Allan celebrated the 60th anniversary of *City of Truro's* 100 mile an hour record by running a high speed special to Plymouth. Here No 4079 *Pendennis Castle* passes Old Oak Common heading for catastrophe.**

As we rocketed down towards Westbury well into the 90s, Bill Thorley started to get anxious. 'We are going too fast,' he kept repeating but, of course, could do nothing about it. Then suddenly there was an almighty brake application and the train shuddered to an awe-inspiring halt. Furiously Bill Andress descended from the footplate as Richards descended from the train. Shouted Bill, 'Some bloody fool's pulled the cord.' 'Yes,' said Richards, 'that bloody fool is me. You've set the train on fire.'

Sure enough the enthusiastic locomen had got their fire so hot to maintain their head of steam that the fire bar had melted and red hot coal and metal had ignited the lower regions of the front coach. After a long delay, we hobbled into Westbury where *Pendennis Castle* was ignominiously removed to be replaced by a dirty 'Hall' which had been doing the morning's shunting and to everyone's amazement gave a spirited run to Taunton where we collected the stand-by 'Castle' and went on uneventfully to Plymouth.

On the way back Jack Hancock took over at Bristol as did the publicity machinery. The BBC had arranged a light aircraft to film the train doing its ton and we all settled back for the spectacular. Alas, it did not happen. We only made 96mph but the BBC used the film and we all got the publicity we wanted despite a growling Bill Andress who continually averred that if he had been on the footplate, *Clun Castle* would have been whipped up to 100mph *at least*.

Another exciting trip created a record in 1966 when we managed to run a train from Paddington to Penzance, the only train ever to have covered the 305 miles without pausing for breath, and returning, also non-stop, from Penzance to Waterloo via the SR route. Diesel locos provided the motive power and went so well that most of the party were able to make the journey by helicopter to the Scilly Isles and back while the train was serviced at Penzance. On the return journey, the aim was almost defeated by a signal check at the approach to the Royal Albert Bridge at Saltash but the driver did his stuff and crept along the platform until the signal cleared and on arrival back at Waterloo our mission was accomplished.

We had tremendous fun organising these rail excursions and something always went awry especially if we ran Pullman cars, many of which must at that time have been in a fairly poor state of health. On one occasion we arrived at Salisbury when the first course of dinner had just been served, two Pullmans had run hot and had to be removed from the train prontissimo so two coachfuls of first class Pullman diners suddenly found themselves out on the platform whilst their dinners were rapidly propelled into the siding and they returned to Waterloo foodless, hungry and very cross huddled in a hastily commandeered SO.

*Above:*
**The special non-stop excursion from Paddington to Penzance crossing the Teign Bridge on the approach to Newton Abbot. The locomotive is No D1010 *Western Campaigner*.** *C. H. S. Owen*

*Below:*
**The 'Pennine Pullman' approaching South Ruislip Junction and about to pass under the Western Region Paddington-Birmingham main line on 12 May 1956. The train is headed by 'A4' 4-6-2 No 60014 *Silver Link*.**

*Above:*
**The newly found travel shop at Horsham.**

*Below:*
**One of the first 'shoe-string' Ian Allan Travel shops in the shadow of the castle at Windsor.**

*Above:*
**Shoestring operation. An early Ian Allan Travel branch.**

*Below:*
**In the midst of the big boys, Ian Allan Travel at Farnborough.**

On another Pullman excursion, the kitchens ran out of gas and a special trip into Wath yard was necessitated to get at a gas tank wagon to refuel, by which time the lights had failed and our old friend, U. A. Vincent, who always travelled on our specials, was despatched on arrival at Sheffield to purchase as many candles as he could buy. He returned and distributed these candles and probably thereby we created another record of the only candle lit supper ever provided on BR though I shudder to think what the modern Health and Safety Executive would say about nakedly lit candles standing on wooden tables in dried up wooden coaches. The greatest cock-up was yet to come but not till 1982 so I will leave that for the moment.

The Swiss Tourist office in London approached us with regard to the possibility of organising some rail-oriented trips to Switzerland, their Herren Kunz and Klee were enthusiastic collaborators and provided the most magnificent tours I have ever participated in. Reserved first class accommodation was tacked on to every train we travelled on and opportunities were given such as could never happen here. Our train stopped once in the middle of a spiral tunnel and the passengers invited to alight, the train went ahead whilst the passengers, illuminated only by flares carried by a few SBB men slithered and slipped over the oily sleepers to regain the daylight some 20 minutes later. On another occasion the train stopped on the main Bernese Oberland line so that we could disentrain to view the infant Rhone from the top of an unguarded precipice.

But there was a more serious side to 'Travel' than playing at rail excursions which when one took into consideration the unseen overheads were probably at best only marginally economic. There was always drama when train formations did not turn up as arranged and the seat reservations all went wrong. Everyone always asked for a seat down-side corner facing the engine, we did our best but if BR got the vehicles wrong, they often finished up up-side back to the engine. And bitterly complained. The Travel company had continued to expand. Dennis Williams introduced us to Farenwide Travel at Hayes, a small go-ahead business which specialised in school parties as well as retail sales. They were fairly easily assimilated and added a new dimension to the company which was developing, as is our wont, serendipitously. One of our Shepperton staff moved to Alton and encouraged us to fill in a blank there whilst the spot was vacant. We did. On a suggestion from BR, the Company Secretary was despatched to Basingstoke to find suitable premises in this developing area. He failed but came back with a shop at Salisbury. One day I returned from a trip to Chichester with the MD of 'Travel', drove through Christ's Hospital to show him the School and in going through Horsham town saw an empty shop with a 'To Let' board up. We took it. Thus eventually we built up the chain.

Lots of other people were getting in on the rail excursion act and as so much effort was required in the organisation it seemed pointless to compete in a profitless market. Trevor Bailey decided to go further afield organising a deluxe tour to South Africa which was much enjoyed by the participants but not much use to anyone else. Trevor, however, enjoyed it and set about organising another. It was here that he and I fell out. He insisted on going ahead and I made it conditional that he did not accompany the party. He did and on his return there was no alternative but to suggest he did his stuff elsewhere. Which he accepted with a good grace and we kept in touch regularly until his sudden death in 1991. He had been the founder of our Travel company and enthusiastically though completely uncommercially developed it, and while he was there and after he left, it took a long, long time for the accountants to make any sense of it.

*Above:*
**After railway excursions why not some aircraft trips? Here is the first Ian Allan flight by BEA Trident Two.**

*Above left:*
**Ian Allan rail tour to South Wales branches rolls gently into Crumlin station.**

*Above:*
**An Ian Allan rail tour to Plymouth called at Totnes for a trip by the Dart Valley line to Buckfastleigh on 2 October 1965.**

*Left:*
**'Merchant Navy' Class No 35028 *Clan Line* passing through Sonning cutting with a Swindon rail tour on 21 April 1965.**

89

*Right:*
**Pendennis Castle heads for Worcester on
8 August 1965.** *Paul Riley*

*Below:*
**Locospotters investigate the complicated
operations at Eastleigh Works.**

*Below right:*
**Rail tour at Darlington North Road on 3 October
1964.**

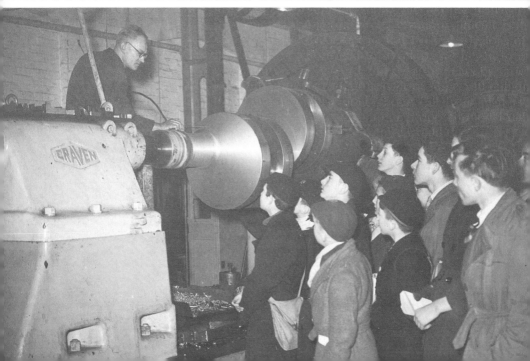

*Above:*
**Flying Scotsman** **goes west with an all-Pullman rail tour emerging from Twerton Tunnel, Bath, in 1963.**

*Below:*
**Silver Jubilee: a friendlier face than that of Stanley Raymond was shown by No 7029** *Clun Castle* **as it climbed out of Copenhagen Tunnel with the Ian Allan Silver Jubilee celebration train to York in 1967.**

*Above:*
**Youthful enthusiasts explore the inside of Eastleigh works.**

*Below:*
**On the Somerset & Dorset, 'Schools' Class No 30932 *Blundells* piloting 4-4-0 No 40601 are pictured standing at Radstock en route for Bath Green Park on 26 April 1954.** *E. D. Bruton*

*Above:*
**In April 1958 the lads were taken to Ashford Works and the Romney Hythe & Dymchurch Railway. The train is headed here by 'Schools' Class No 30908 *Westminster*.**

*Above right:*
**2-6-0 No 6384 entering Bath Green Park with a special train from Paddington, Severn Tunnel Junction and Severn Bridge — the 'Severn and Wessex Express — on 14 May 1960. In the background ex-S&DJR 2-8-0 No 53807 waits to haul the special south to Bournemouth.**

*Right:*
**A special from Charing Cross to Ashford and then from Redhill through Eastleigh back to Waterloo on 5 April 1961.** *J. Scrace*

*Above:*

**Modified 'Merchant Navy' Class locomotive No 35023 *Holland-Afrika Line* arriving at Exeter St David's station with the Ian Allan excursion during the return journey on 20 September 1958.**

*Below:*

**Western Region 'Castle' Class 4-6-0 No 7029 *Clun Castle* ascending the Lickey Bank with the Ian Allan rail tour on 27 March 1965.**

*Above right:*

**'Fenlands Express' headed by Class 7 Pacific No 70000 *Britannia* at Liverpool Street.**

*Below right:*

**Further on the train arrives at South Lynn now headed by 'B12' 4-6-0 No 61530.**

*Above:*
**West Country excursion crossing Meldon Viaduct.**

*Above right:*
**Ian Allan marked the end of through services from London to Birkenhead by running the 'Birkenhead Flyer' on 4 March 1967.**

*Right:*
**The itinerary was so popular that a second train, entitled 'The Zulu', was run on the same day but on a different route, each train going out one way and returning the other.** *Pendennis Castle* **and** *Clun Castle* **did the honours.**

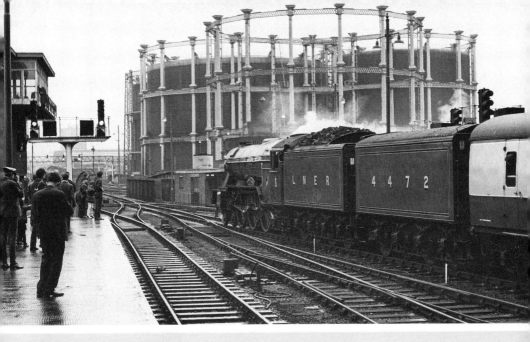

*Above left:*
**'Pennine Pullman' leaves Todmorden.**

*Above:*
**The 'Brontë Rail Tour': No 4472 waiting to leave St Pancras on 23 March 1968. Note the double tender for maximum water capacity.**

*Left:*
**The 'Daffodil Express' heads for Wales behind No 4472 *Flying Scotsman*.**

*Left:*
**A visit to the Midland Railway. A double-headed special gets away from Buxton.**

*Below left:*
**BR Standard Class '9F' 2-10-0 No 92220 *Evening Star* is seen on arrival at Paddington with an Ian Allan special from Southampton on 3 April 1964.**

*Above:*
**A 1964 special from Paddington to Doncaster headed by No 46163.**

*Below:*
**Waiting to leave Marylebone, No 60014 *Silver Link* heads the 'Pennine Pullman' whilst Cecil J. Allen discusses the situation with a fellow enthusiast.**

# 9

# Chichester and Coombelands

As the retirement of Hilda Harmer had approached, we decided we needed a professional Company Secretary to take over the accounts and Kenn Groves was duly appointed. I taught him not to wear brown suede shoes to the office or drink brown ale in a cocktail bar and he very soon became my righthand man. But he did not like doing accounts and found himself other niches. After the retirement of Harmer, slowly but surely we began to get in a mess.

My masonic career had taken me through the chair of the Lodge in 1965 and I became friendly with the Secretary who was a real numbers man and had recently retired. He came to help us out and by the time he had finished, we were in a bigger mess than ever. Our auditor, Roy Mace, came in with a degree of urgency not previously witnessed, 'Do something quickly or within six weeks you will be in real trouble.' It was then that Norman Miles came on the scene; he had just returned from Rhodesia with his family having deemed it prudent to get out while the going was reasonably good and was acting as a consultant. Norman was a very professional chartered accountant and I asked him first to look at our Printing company. He stated his terms, said he would take a few days to take in the situation and that if he felt it required his services, there would be no fee until he was commissioned. He went off and far from taking a few days, he was back in about five minutes to endorse Mace's view. He reorganised the accounting system of that company and then went on to do the rest. 'This will take me six months and I'll be out of a job.' That was in 1971, he retired (partially) in 1990.

David and Paul had now done their stint at prep school in Walton on Thames and moved off to Seaford College where they both did reasonably well in their O levels - only perhaps because three O levels admitted them to the 6th Form Club where there was a bar. From school they went to Guildford Technical College where they did very little other than select their future wives. David then went to W. H. Smiths to learn how to be a bookseller and, therefore, a publisher. WHS were very good to him and trained him well. Paul was to be apprenticed to another travel operator which at the crucial moment got itself taken over and he was left to serve his early days within the IA Group, in fact learning how to sweep the floor in the print factory before graduating to stamping brochures with Ian Allan Travel's name and address. Ultimately they both became established members of the company and began the inevitable and inexorable process of ousting the old man.

Sadly at this time the old man was having a bumpy ride with the National Westminster bank, at the Shepperton branch of which a new manager had arrived. He took the view that they should have some security for providing an overdraft facility of a few hundred thousand pounds. I disagreed and refused to accommodate him. The bust up resulted in the area manager asking me to go and see him. I suggested he should come and see me, which he did and got himself so excited that he almost stretched himself halfway across my desk to hammer home his point.

Alas, it was all too much for the poor chap; that night he had a coronary and was off work for six months. So, rather than destroy any more NWB personnel, I went to see the local Barclays manager (good old Rotary Club!) who welcomed the Group with open arms and Barclays have gone on welcoming us ever since. And I highly recommend them!

I now come back to the Rotary Club connection, for Alf Pitfield, who had been masterminding the construction of 10¼in locomotives, decided he wanted to move out of his building in the station yard at Shepperton — a 5,000sq ft single storey concrete factory he had virtually built by his own fair hand, sweat and blood. We did a deal with him, took over his factory or, rather, his lease with BR, and moved our growing printing concern from its specially constructed but restricted accommodation at Terminal House into a new home and we hope aptly named it Pitfield House.

So by 1971 we were firmly installed at Shepperton with our publishing and travel operations at Terminal House and printing at Pitfield House. The facilities for storage and packing and despatch were becoming impossibly tight and we decided to move out of the area to cheaper and more commodious premises. On holiday in Sussex John Cannon and I stumbled on a brand new warehouse complex in Chichester and decided to take one of the units. So our entire warehouse was moved lock, stock and barrel down to Chichester where a new local staff were recruited. Invoices and delivery notes were still produced at Shepperton, posted down to Chichester and despatched as promptly as possible though the 50-mile gap in location did cause problems of communication.

The move to Shepperton which sparked off so many diversifications led me away from my original publishing role and as the markets got harder and competition increased I found myself rather more inclinded towards developing new ventures which were much more exciting. We had a good

# Chichester and Coombelands

*Above:*
**A very spick and span printshop at Pitfield House, Shepperton.**

*Below:*
**Outside the packing station at Chichester.**

106

*Above:*
**Busy scene in the packing and despatch department at Chichester.**

*Below:*
**The interior of Coombelands when first taken over by Ian Allan Printing.**

team in place headed by Geoffrey Allen and now joined by Norman Miles who had virtually fallen into the shoes of Willie Brett who died (conveniently) on the last day of our financial year 30 November 1968, leaving everything neat and tidy. They were joined by Alan Hollingsworth, a Group Captain newly retired from a NATO role and who led us into our militaria list with particular accent naturally on matters aeronautical. I think my only contribution was to interfere, worry about the economics and generally make life difficult for everyone.

The sales team was the best any publisher could have wished for and recruited from very different quarters. Eddie Rogers had been a tram inspector at Kingston and transferred to trolleybuses. In his spare time he did a bit of gardening for my mother: just like Jack Deller before him he came in to help with the packing and landed up as foreman, a job he did with distinction for many years before he too joined the sales force 'on the road' covering the south of England most efficiently. Our oldest inhabitant, Ron Cooke, covered the north from Leeds: Les Gibson had been recruited from the *News of the World* organisation and found selling quite a change from girlie magazines whilst John Funnell covered the Midlands. They all put in many years of active service and, indeed, Ron Cooke and John Funnell only retired during 1992.

Our publishing list expanded into a much wider range and under Alan Hollingsworth an entirely new series of coloured coffee table books on the beauties of the countryside evolved and we launched a separate company Town & County Books Ltd to market them. The photographers were Dutch, the printers were German-speaking Italians and none of us had any common language with them so we had to use interpretation. It was really quite remarkable that anything ever happened as the meetings were all totally unintelligible.

Around this time another extraordinary affair occurred. We had for some time done business with a local printer — The Press at Coombelands at Addlestone. They were an offshoot of Benn Brothers whose main function was to produce their parent publisher's large range of technical magazines: jobbing work was taken in to fill in the holes in the production line and our paperback books suited their machinery. The entire plant was old-fashioned hot metal typesetting and letterpress machinery, becoming rapidly outdated by the onset of litho processes. Just before Christmas Tony Fisher, their MD, rang up to make an appointment. Cautiously I asked whether he was coming to sell us his services to which he replied negatively. When he actually arrived he said it was not his services he wanted to sell but the whole shooting match. The 'Press' had been created in 1926 and combined not only a large factory area fronted by a mock Tudor block of offices and flats but also an entire estate of houses in which the happy workers lived

*Above:*
**A new era at Coombelands. Derick Sharp, managing director of Ian Allan Printing Ltd, formally accepts the key from the vendor's representative.**

*Above:*
**The splendid mock Tudor façade to the printing factory at Coombelands.**

*Below:*
**When times get really hard and the staff all go home, the directors have to get down and work themselves. A pre-Christmas scene at Coombelands with Kenn Groves, Mollie Allan, Alan Hollingsworth and David Allan trying to catch up with the Christmas trade in 1979.**

and a social club for them to recreate in. It was, in fact, a mini-suburb covering a huge acreage.

The thought of taking this lot on was formidable and in my mind I dismissed it, whilst Mr Fisher went on talking persuasively. Benn Bros had decided to close the factory and obviously had a huge redundancy and union problem to face so they sought to find a locally based publisher/printer who could take the whole lot over without too much redundancy. The asking price was not the greatest of their priorities for their concern was for a peaceable and not too expensive withdrawal. The housing estate of very pleasant residences had been a great idea for holding staff to the 'Press' when they were in the category of tied cottages but the Rent Act had blown that little ploy out of the water and many of the houses were let on low rents to former employees who had departed to go into more lucrative jobs leaving their landlords with rather a poor return on their capital value. It was mutually decided that the 'Estate' would be ruled out of the deal and the properties were afterwards separately dealt with.

We had to come to a fairly speedy decision and visitation of the premises, in order not to set off rumours, had to be covert — so covert, in fact, that the formal inspection was arranged for Boxing Day when Norman Miles, Derick Sharp, (our Printing MD) and I met Tony Fisher clandestinely in a sub-zero temperature factory. It was much too large, much too old-fashioned, much too expensive, much too cold, in fact, much too everything for me.

But the next day I was confronted by an enthusiastic Norman Miles whose eyes were bright with £ signs as a good business deal and an equally enthusiastic Derick Sharp who saw the whole project as a huge empire building move. There was a factory area of 41,000ft in over two acres of land. The great advantage of bringing up our warehouse and distribution arrangements to be under one roof with the print factory was attractive, as was cutting the 50 miles between Shepperton and Chichester to just four between Shepperton and Coombelands. We decided to go ahead though we could not fulfil all the desires of the 'Press' for our staffing levels were nothing compared with those available but some staff were retained and have been with us ever since.

From time to time our beloved bankers invite our directors to lunch at local head office and it was shortly after the Coombelands affair began that we were summoned to Windsor by the local directors, the chief of whom was Alan Simms who was a railway enthusiast and avid supporter of Southampton FC. Fortunately I had been to the 'Dell' so could talk to him in his own language. In the course of conversation I mentioned our intended purchase and casually asked him whether he would be kind enough to supply the money. Without hesitation he just replied, 'Of course.' 'What, no strings?' I asked and he said, 'Certainly not.' And thereby confirmed a delightfully happy relationship we have always enjoyed with Barclays who have never failed to agree to any of our requests and never mentioned the words 'security' or 'collateral' though they have unfortunately considered it necessary to ask for interest on loans which *we* think is a bit unnecessary!

So the deal was done and we became the proud owners of The Press at Coombelands, or rather the major part of it for during the war the Press had sold about one-third of the original factory premises to Calor Gas who remained in occupation of the lower end of the estate whilst we fell heir to an entire road round our perimeter of the property.

The Chichester operation was transferred to Coombelands as was the entire printing company from Shepperton and its former premises, Pitfield House, were sub-let on a long lease to a local engineering firm. Our 'Graphics' section now had two bases — Publishing at Terminal House, Shepperton and Printing and Distribution at Coombelands.

*Above:*
**Books galore to all parts of the world were despatched from Coombelands.**

# 10

# Hotels

I had always had a yen to have a hotel and I envisaged something fairly small but upmarket by the sea with a private beach and not too far away. We searched high and low and learnt a lot about hotels. The disgusting kitchens and foul food storage arrangements really opened our eyes and we began to despair of even finding the right place. The Cannons' connection with Knight Frank & Rutley had caused them to feed some 'selected' premises to us and one such was at Broadway. My son Paul, then aged 14, and I were returning from somewhere and decided to divert via Broadway: we had lunch and rather liked the place but dismissed it as being just about as far from the sea as it is possible to get in England. On returning from another fruitless hotel visit, a posse of us decided to have another look at Broadway, Mollie fell in love with the place at first sight and we all decided we liked it and did the deal.

Our experiences of hotel management could fill an entire book — of horror stories — all the things you hear about hotels have happened to us. It is a quite unbelievable world of thieves and vagabonds, queers and crooks. Not just the staff but customers too, in fact more so.

The Broadway Hotel *had* two stars from the AA/RAC and was obviously run on a shoe string. The manageress, Phyl Richards, operated on strictly economic grounds ensuring maximum profitability from all her guests. The sofa and some of the armchairs in the lounge were propped up on bricks and the vegetable content of the diners' menu was unexceptionally tinned diced carrots, turnips and peas. We set about the long and laborious task of changes and improvements. We built new bedrooms and found that running an hotel is very similar to owning a Hornby train set: it is never complete, always changes, always improvements, always refurbishment. It never stops. But undeterred we decided to have three more hotels and when one came up at nearby Evesham, we bought it, refurbished it, restaffed it but could not make a go of it. By now we had two male managers, one at Broadway and one at Evesham, they were at daggers drawn with each other and on one occasion reverted to actual fisticuffs at 7 o'clock in the morning when one besieged the other's house, shouting at him to come out and fight.

*Above:*
**An unusual attempt at diversification was the acquisition of the village store in Laleham in 1981 as an adjunct to the hotel company. Although business was brisk, the opposition of the supermarkets was too much and the building was converted into four rather nice residential flats.**

*Below:*
**Evesham Hotel.**

With the Evesham Hotel we acquired a wonderful chef whose speciality was salmon in every conceivable form and which was almost always on the menu as he could obtain it at very favourable rates. We had a party at home one day and my wife requested that he send up a dressed salmon. That very highly moral chartered accountant, Norman Miles, kindly collected this on one of his visits to the hotel and nursed it home for us on his lap. It was terrific and everyone much enjoyed it and so did I until a few weeks later a clipping arrived from the local Evesham paper reporting that aforesaid chef had just been convicted of large scale salmon poaching.

Then there was the complaint by one of the chambermaids that as she went to bed one night the manager stepped out of her wardrobe and attempted to make love to her; a knife wielding event by the assistant chef — so what's new? — was also recorded. There was the porter who in a fit of pique took to urinating on all the maids' beds and finally locked himself in his room for a week and was only finally deposed when we cut off his electricity and literally froze him out.

For some unearthly reason I bought a double decker bus from John Evans who, apart from being a Dart Valley director, was also an architect and who had redesigned the Evesham Hotel. It was a Bristol Lodekka and in very good nick and we decided to have a Christmas programme based on both hotels with the historic bus to convey the punters from one to the other. There was a bit of a rave-up going on on Christmas Eve at Broadway with the bus standing on the forecourt when I was summoned to reception to be confronted by a police sergeant and constable who first said we were breaking the law by playing music and despite reassurances that all the revellers were residents, decided that I spoke not the truth, which I did. They then wanted to know all about the bus which I explained — also adding that it was 11.55 on Christmas Eve and did they really have to be so officious? The bus they said was illegal as it had no PSV licence: it was not a PSV but a private vehicle and was properly licensed and I told them so. It only has one tail light. Buses only need one tail light. Ah, they jumped in, but you said this was not a bus and as a private 'car' it needs two tail lights. Out came the book, pencils were licked and the constabulary and I withdrew to the car park to inspect aforesaid offending bus. To all our amazements the bus had disappeared: the case for the prosecution collapsed and I reported the vehicle stolen.

Actually it had not been stolen but the malevolent manager of Evesham had driven the bus back there empty in order to embarrass the Broadway manager who would have to find some other way of returning his guests to Evesham at 1am on a Christmas morning.

That was not the only encounter with the police. One fine day two plain clothes detectives confronted the manager, 'We have reason to believe you are harbouring stolen property on the premises.' 'Indeed we are not,' was her stern reply. The coppers then brought in a chap in handcuffs who directed the cortege to one of the bedrooms, the side of the bath was removed to uncover an enormous cache of stolen silver. Then there was the lady who came across from the 'Lygon Arms' bringing with her a television set and receiving a constant stream of male visitors. When eventually pursued by the manager she took refuge in the lavatory where she remained for three hours on the pretext that she was constipated. The tv set had been stolen from the 'Lygon' and she had obviously set up in business in her room for 'personal services'.

Spare blankets, pillows, rain umbrellas all vanish with unabated regularity; it seems that guests are not now content with just pinching the coat hangers and salt cellars. One night the safe disappeared and on another a beautiful antique grandfather clock walked out and on both there were no signs of entry. The police picked up the thief of the grandfather clock in Taunton of all places, but the clock had long since been 'fenced'. We sold the Evesham Hotel which we suspect was haunted as we met with several very unaccountable manifestations. I don't think I believe in ghosts but there was something very funny about that place. We carried on with Broadway which is also allegedly slightly haunted and which has been a great pleasure and a most interesting business to develop. It goes on from strength to strength though we are not contemplating completing our plan to acquire three more! But Broadway does now have three stars and we think it is now quite good!

We had a few further forays into the catering business through the hotel company. John Evans discovered some ancient warehouses at Padstow and being interested in the area and an architect, formed a triumvirate with me and, of all people, a retired tax inspector, which bought the property and converted it into good harbourside residential property. My third share consisted of a shop and three tall thin houses which were let regularly as self-catering accommodation. We also acquired the 'local shop' in Laleham. We turned it into a mini supermarket and it did very well, though the overheads, coupled with substantial pilferage from people who had always seemed so respectable, ultimately decided us to fold it up. It was nice while it lasted.

# 11

# Mystic Arts

Earlier there was mention of the masonic connection and this came again serendipitously to influence our lives in 1971. Our auditor, Roy Mace, also acted for a firm known as A Lewis (Masonic Publishers) Ltd. This was run by a Teddy London aged 78 and his nephew Chris Beach then in his early twenties. Quite apparently they did not get on too well for they were as different as chalk and cheese. London was a hard drinking, hard smoking, hard gambling tearaway whilst Chris was a quiet, hardworking and somewhat introverted young chap. We came to an extraordinary deal. London had a sick wife, a little older than he and an even more sickly daughter, both of whom he was anxious to provide for in the event of his shuffling off this mortal coil before them; he wanted to retire and we agreed to take over the shares in his company for a down payment but with guaranteed pen-

*Above:*
**Ian Allan Regalia was closely involved with the 275th anniversary of the United Grand Lodge of England at Earl's Court on 10 June 1992.**

sions for him and on his demise his wife and daughter. At his age it looked a reasonable deal; he drove a car like a fiend round busy London streets, rode a horse regularly and by every rule in the book should have been at the Pearly gates long before the age of 80. It all happened in reverse order, his daughter died, then his wife who would both have had smaller pensions, but he went on for ever - almost. In fact, he reached 92 before releasing us from our contract by falling off his twig.

With uncle out of the business, 14 years earlier Chris Beach had blossomed into an enthusiastic manager and subsequently director of the company. From fairly abstruse masonic books and rituals we were now selling regalia and jewels of all sorts. We moved from the Lewis premises we had acquired in Earls Court and concentrated our effort at Shepperton. We started a new periodical called *Masonic Square* which one of our own Lodge members, Ben Hutton, edited and ran from scratch for 15 years before handing over at the age of 79 to a younger man. A Lewis — note the lack of a full point between the A and the L — meant exactly that — a lewis — for the founder had been the son of a mason just as I had been. We later decided to bring the company in line with the rest of the Group and changed the name to Ian Allan Regalia Ltd but retaining the monicker 'Lewis Masonic' for publicity and imprint purposes and to retain the old connection. We also inherited the 100-year old 'Baskerville Press'.

So fast did the company expand that it was decided to acquire manufacturing premises in the 'embroidery' area of Leicestershire and opened up at Hinckley in September 1986 where a skilled team produce all forms of masonic, military, corporate and club regalia items. Masonry is worldwide and the amount of export business generated through this company is very considerable indeed and many an overseas Grand Lodge obtains its appurtenances from Ian Allan Regalia.

# 12

# An Unfortunate Diversion

Now for something completely different. I have always been something of a football supporter and eventually with our teenage sons, John Cannon and I became season ticket holders at Chelsea. On Saturdays when they were playing away, I would wander down to watch Staines Town in the Isthmian League. The smell of my interest in the round ball reached across the river to Walton where Walton & Hersham FC were in some sort of problem. Under the redoubtable Alan Batsford's management, the Club had scaled the dizzy heights and won the FA Amateur Cup at Wembley. Alan Batsford moved off to Wimbledon to work his wonders there and left Walton & Hersham somewhat leaderless and impoverished.

Norman Miles, I and another distinguished Walton resident, and a director of the Trusthouse Forte outfit were invited on to the Board which we blandly accepted not realising what lay ahead. It all seemed so nice and cosy at the time, seats in the directors' box and an after match lush up with visiting officials but it did not turn out like that at all: it was a grinding and overpowering worry from beginning to end and one wonders why anyone anywhere wants to get involved in such a tough industry. And this was only amateur stuff.

Two of the original club-directors remained on the Board and for my sins, I was made Chairman. The first problem we hit was that the players wanted to be paid, notwithstanding that they were amateurs, obviously shamateurs. The pay must not be apparent, nor taxed: it was the old syndrome of pound notes appearing, surprise, surprise, in the players' football boots. This was too much for Norman's Chartered Accountant status and ethics and for me and my Forte colleague. We then looked at other sources of revenue for the Club; someone, actually one of the directors, was running a professionally operated big prize weekly draw. We asked for details of how it was run and what the revenue was: answer came there none, it was none of our business and we must be grateful for what *pourboires* came from it. We looked at the catering department: how was it financed, what profit did it make? Answers again came there none. Keep out, we do it very nicely thank you. We looked at the drinks cabinet in the Board and yes, we did get an answer here, '*You* pay for them'. We looked at the 'gate' facilities and did not like the control there either.

So we were very unhappy at the business side of the operation and we could see money going out of the window into a lot of vested pockets whilst Norman ascertained that the Inland Revenue *did* want to know about payments to players and did have a few enquiries to make about past history.

I never realised I could worry so much about a game of football: we appointed a new manager who tried very hard but the team's ability to get balls in the net failed to come up to scratch and the crowd started to get nasty. We lost game after game and I sweated buckets as we went down in the league table and down the drain at every match. The Club was losing money which we found we were having to finance and eventually we decided that far from having fun, we were worrying ourselves skinny and having to pay for the unpleasure. The awful truth dawned that none of the three recruited 'outside' directors were cut out for the job and we tendered our resignations.

We got quite a lot of stick from the local sports reporters for abandoning the ship but even if we ratted at least we saved ourselves from being drowned rats and the club eventually recovered and lived to fight another day — and so do we.

One little side incident of the Walton & Hersham saga was a contact with a commander at Scotland Yard who invited Norman and me to go and visit the Black Museum. We duly turned up at around 10am where we were greeted by the great man and handed over to the museum curator who looked after us admirably and absorbingly for an hour or so. At the conclusion of our museum tour we were taken back to the commanders' floor where our host offered us a drink; at that moment another commander appeared and a discussion took place as to whose bottle was used. Suffice it to say that for the next hour or so bottles appeared from bottom drawers like there was no tomorrow — exactly as seen on tv. I don't like whisky and vice versa, Norman was better at it than I was but anyway, we had expected to see the museum and be on our way back within a couple of hours and my car was on a two hour meter. That was no problem we were informed — drink up and have another. There was no escape, lunch was laid on, and thankful at the prospect of some proverbial blotting paper, we headed for the trough. But no, we were off to 'The Tank' which if my memory serves me aright, is a vast bar in the bowels of the Yard to which the troops withdraw for refreshment, so before we were fed we had to sink a couple of pints which was all very disconcerting. After lunch we staggered round to see the Traffic Division at work and very interesting it was, I think, for really all we needed was fresh air.

We got out at 4pm and drove back to the office and that evening I was booked to go to our Bracknell Travel office to entertain the staff to dinner as a reward for their achieving the best results of all the branches. I managed to get to Bracknell and sink a large tomato juice, I then quickly withdrew and just got home as my stomach decided it had had enough and rejected its unwelcome contents. I don't think I have ever been so ill before or since and studiously avoid all contact with policemen bearing bottles.

*Above:*
**The Ian Allan ladies' football team of 1970 — at least two of the front row still survive 'in harness' to tell the tale.**

# 13

# Railway Personalities

My own personal function in the Group was beginning to change radically. I had started as a publisher of railway books because I liked publishing and I liked railways. I enjoyed the rough and tumble of bargaining with printers and doing sales deals with customers and no-one believed me when one day I announced I had decided to hand over the buying of print to others. Of course, no-one has ever done it properly ever since and they all have the greatest difficulty in getting me to keep my nose out of publishing. Way back Geoffrey Allen, who had become MD of Ian Allan Ltd, our publishing company, told me that the MD's job was impossible as long as I was around. Twenty years later my son David told me the same thing. Perhaps they were both right. Anyway, fortunately for all of them I had other fish to fry. Setting up the travel company involved finding the right shops which was my job. Kenn Groves as Company Secretary then had to do the necessary formalities of acquisition and basic shop fitting and we then handed the whole thing over to the Travel management to get on with. In fact, once a new shop was open, all Kenn and I had to do was to visit it occasionally just to show we were still interested but I had to be the 'front' man although it was not a role I particularly enjoyed; public speaking and appearances were never my forte and I always preferred to leave that to other people.

Geoffrey Allen and I had struck up an acquaintance with Gerry Fiennes when he was Line Manager Great Northern at King's Cross and maintained our links with him until he reached the apex of his career as General Manager Eastern Region. We talked him into writing his autobiography which he called *I Tried to Run a Railway* (qv if you can find one). Fiennes was a very outspoken chap and he did not much care for the heirarchy at 222 Marylebone Road. He was an awe-inspiring man and I never really felt comfortable in his presence but he was useful to us and we basked in the reflected glory of being on friendly terms with him.

As the book was about to be published the balloon went up. Stanley Raymond was chairman of the BRB, Eric Merrill was his Public Relations Adviser and they did not like one iota some of the things Fiennes had included in the book and tried to make us suppress it. We were too far down the road to hold publication and out it came. Our publicity machine had fed a few choice extracts to the press and they were headlined on many front pages.

Fiennes was sacked on the spot.

Now, as luck would have it, that very week was our 25th Anniversary and we had organised a dinner at the Royal Hotel, Paddington at which Sir Stanley Raymond and Lady ditto were our principal guests. They turned up and Raymond totally and deliberately ignored me throughout the preprandial refreshment and at the dinner table where he sat on my right. After half an hour I asked him whether he intended to keep this attitude up all the evening, to which he snapped, 'I've got nothing to thank you for, you've got me the sack.' That was news to me. Barbara Castle, the Minister of Transport, had that day fired him. I had a very unpleasant celebration for our 25th Anniversary at which Raymond made a thoroughly offensive speech and complained bitterly that not all the diners were guests and that Lady Raymond had not received a bouquet. Thus the desecrator of Brunel and the de-Great Westerniser of Paddington got his come-uppance. He did not survive. We did.

*Above:*
**Charles Hemmings, centre, organises a display with a senior WHS manager to promote *I Tried to Run a Railway*.**

We felt a bit guilty about the sacking of Gerry Fiennes though he quickly took a directorship with a well-known company in the north and much to my delight, accepted an invitation to come on to our Board. He was not my cup of tea and nor was a small growing company his. I took him one day on a tour of our burgeoning Travel empire of which I was very proud and on our return, asked his views of it. 'Not bad for a shoestring operation,' was his summation of the day. Of course, he was right but he put it so bluntly that it was totally unacceptable. After attending a few Board meetings, he slowly faded away, he never actually resigned and still kept in touch making several contributions to our magazines and then sadly he died and an era ended, an era of successful entrepreneurial railway management, the like of which has not been seen since apart from the notable exceptions of Chris Green and John Prideaux.

Fiennes and his opposite number W. G. (Willie) Thorpe, Line Manager Great Eastern, who later aspired to general managership, Alan Pegler, Eric Treacy, L. T. C. Rolt, Cecil, Pat Whitehouse, Ossie Nock, Hamilton Ellis, George Dow, Derek Barrie were all great chaps in their day and most of

*Above:*
**Progress chasing on the Great Eastern in 1960 prior to the departure of a special train to Harwich. Left to right: C. J. Allen, D. A. Farrell (PRO), Ian Allan and Hamilton Ellis.**

them had become personal friends and formed a great phalanx in the growing enthusiasm for railways as the locospotters of the 1940s and 1950s came to adulthood. These chaps all contributed to my own widening interest in life in general.

Life, of course, is greatly influenced by the people you come across in it and I count myself fortunate at the wide spectrum of characters with whom my meanderings have brought me into contact. Relatives and close non-business friends whom I value most highly I keep out of these comments as I have to go on living with them but who are, of course, the backbone of life.

My business philosophy is simple and not very original but I do try to practise it. The customer is always right. If we provide a commodity or service with which the customer is unhappy it has to be rectified or the money returned in full. I always work on that premise and always deal personally with complaints sent to me. I fervently believe that if a complaint is handled properly the complainant will become a good future customer and a great advocate. Here are some observations of people who have left their metaphorical marks on me and, therefore, our company(ies). First there was Cuthbert Grasemann, the Southern PRO, a bully and an unreasonable stinker yet he was a chap we all looked up to. He was unquestionably the boss and his staff trembled when he raged and we all moved on to cloud nine where we basked in the sunshine of his smiles — even if he just said 'good morning' in the toilet, for most people he totally ignored. I think he did influence me to the extent that when later on I sometimes felt my authority was being undermined I remembered his ability to move into overdrive and crush all opposition and I rather suspect I may do the same myself.

Alistair MacLeod, another senior SR officer when I first met him, was an entirely different cup of tea, though he too could get pretty stroppy when things did not please him. Basically he was a kind, decent chap of whom all his acquaintances and friends were very fond. He and his wife Winifred took us to a G&S production at the Rudolph Steiner Hall by the LM Region Dramatic Society and in the interval the news broke of J. F. Kennedy's assassination earlier in the day. The show was good, the occasion memorable but it was the only time in my 50-year association with ABMacL that he ever entertained me to anything. He was, of course, a Scot but generous of time and effort, a dyed in the wool enthusiast with tremendous skill at model-making, engineering and attention to detail and he was a great wit with the strongest driest sense of humour.

MacLeod led me directly to Cecil J. Allen who became my guide, philosopher and friend and obviously at my young age of 22 when I first met him, felt I was in need of care and protection. Although he was careful with his money to the extent of near meanness, he was very uncommercial and would often accept the quick buck rather than speculate for something more later. Perhaps this was due to his strict non-conformist, non-drinking, non-smoking regimen which made him cautious *in extremis*. When he came on to the Board of Ian Allan Ltd his watch words repeatedly recited were *festina lente* which you will know means 'make haste slowly'. If I had accepted all his 'lentiness' I do not think we would have had 'festinaed' anywhere and he certainly got very worried if I had a dig at the railways. When the LMS decided to charge reproduction fees for the use of the photographs I attacked them in print. That brought forth a severe reprimand from Cecil whose view was that such an attack would get me nowhere and that the LMS would treat me as an annoying little fly and swat me accordingly. He was wrong; actually they saw the error of their ways and removed the charge.

But Cecil was a good and staunch friend. Under pressure from Terry Holder he switched his 'Locomotive Practices and Performance' articles for *The Railway Magazine* to *Trains Illustrated/Modern Railways*. He introduced his son Geoffrey to us and wrote innumerable books. He had a strong detestation for Ossie Nock whom he considered as an upstart, muscling in on his 'Locomotive Performance' territory which I think he believed was his alone by divine right. He was with us until the end, indeed he had spent the weekend with GFA at the Broadway Hotel and was on his way home after breakfast in the car when he quietly died on the back seat.

O. J. Morris was eccentric to say the least: he was overweight, unhealthy and a confirmed bachelor, entirely harmless and benevolent. He was a great photographer though it took him hours to take one photograph with an ancient plate camera and tripod covered with the traditional black cloth under which he spent hours in focusing before the actual shot. When we got him involved with the Romney Hythe & Dymchurch Railway, Jack Howey, impatiently watching him under his black cloth, dubbed him 'the Professor' and he was thereafter always known as 'Prof'. He was an excellent journalist and had an intimate knowledge of anything that moved in South London. He was always a great draw at the Model Railway Club exhibitions at Central Hall where we regularly had him on our elaborate stand. On the last evening, rather than have the fag of loading up all the unsold stock we would have a 'sale' during the last hour and a half on the final Saturday evening. This caused great consternation to the other traders whom we were undercutting and to the show organisers because we always created rather a noisy crowd. However, it was our tradition and we always did it through thick and thin and walked away with quite a lot of swag in our canvas bag. OJM went mad one day and started a unilateral sale during the early days of the exhibition as trade was a bit slow. I had to warn him not to but as soon as my back was turned he started off again, even offering some books for a halfpenny because no-one was buying them. As he was a director, none of the staff could really gainsay him so alas this and other very odd goings-on he started doing decided us that it was time for him to retire from the Board. He took it very badly and I am afraid things were never quite the same again. I probably mishandled him as I did several others in my time but this one I always regretted.

Rixon Bucknall was a half colonel in the Guards, spoke with a very large plum in his mouth and produced a series of books on railways. He was a very amiable chap and we ultimately acquired his photographic collection and his publishing rights. My memory fails me and I do not know quite what happened to him but he was a good friend and supporter. All the records of our negotiations with him seem to have disappeared, perhaps in one of those Craven House bonfires.

Pat Whitehouse I have already mentioned and my life with him has had its ups and downs as we have not always seen eye to eye with each other. On the up side I recall coming back towards Cherbourg in my 1937 Vauxhall 12 after a trip with him and his wife Thelma to Brittany in 1950. His car was ahead of ours which suddenly stopped: after five minutes or so PBW returned to find us stranded with very little money and 40 miles from Cherbourg, two hours to catch the ship to Southampton and no other service for four days. He hitched up a tow rope and proceeded to tow us to Cherbourg, alas after a quarter of a down hill mile, our back wheel suddenly overtook us and we grounded in the middle of the road in a pool of oil. The half shaft had gone. To cut a long story short, we found a local one-man garage in the middle of nowhere, the one-man who was a spitting image of Charlie Chaplin came back with just a crowbar and levered us into the side of the road: we loaded all our worldly possessions in the Whitehousemobile and abandoned EML 690 to its fate. We just caught the boat by the skin of our teeth and exactly one month later the AA delivered EML back to us, mended and none the worse for wear and we were eternally grateful to Pat

On the other hand, when we ran a Special from St Pancras to somewhere or other north of St Alban's and chartered *Clun Castle* which was then in Pat's ownership, things were not quite so happy. As *Clun* backed on to the train, our team produced our 'Ian Allan' headboard and asked the driver to affix it to the lamp iron. PBW stepped in and prohibited it. He and I then came into a head-on conflict. My view was that as we had hired the engine and train we could stick what we liked on the front. Pat's view was that it was his engine and he decided what went on the front. The stationmaster was summoned who seemed to be veering his decision towards Whitehouse: my rejoinder was that no headboard, no train; he could cancel it on the spot or we'd refuse to pay for the charter on the basis that our contract

*Above:*
**The *Clun Castle* expedition from St Pancras showing the engine wearing its disputed headboard.**

included display of headboard — although it probably did not. Stationmaster did the only thing railway men know how in a crisis and walked away: Whitehouse eventually relented and here's a picture of the train to prove it and we are still on speaking terms!

There were two other significant Pats. Pat Garland and Pat Ransome-Wallis. The former, a Birmingham chartered accountant, steeped in the mysteries and traditions of the GWR, who I got to know intimately during 20 years or so on the Board of DVLR plc. A quiet deep-thinking chap with the orderly mind of most CAs. I learnt from him the wisdom of sitting through debates quietly listening and saying nothing and moving in at the end with a profound statement which usually summed everything up sensibly and well; something I have never managed to do. I regret I am far too impulsive to practise what he preached and did so well and so calmly.

Pat Ransome-Wallis was a GP in Herne Bay, a dry sardonic chap usually full of woe but good company and a good photographer; I never read any of the words he produced although we published a lot of books for him. We used to make forays together each year usually to the end of the harbour arm at the Eastern Docks at Dover. He had a permit to drive his car to the end where he would settle for the day to watch the ships coming in and out, he always had a timetable of arrivals and departures and berthing arrangements and was a fount of knowledge on the cross-Channel fleets we were watching. On most occasions a dot on the horizon could be identified by reference to the timesheet and as it hovered nearer the unmistakable markings of Sealink, Townsend, P&O, Belgian Marine, ALC would become apparent.

On one occasion he selected a different venue to visit — the Upnor & Chattenden Naval Railway: on our arrival I was a bit put off at the sight of two very rigid sailors in full rig and with fixed bayonets and thought that any attempt to see what was going on would be greeted rather like my 1940s visit to Burgess Hill. Quite undeterred, PR-W approached the sentry and then said, 'I'm Surgeon Cmdr Ransome-Wallis...,' whereupon the sentry immediately presented arms and in a cloud of white blanco called out the guard commander. The next thing we were in the guardroom waiting for a special train to be mustered to take us for a ride. His wife Toosie, also a doctor, died shortly afterwards and it was not much later that Pat diagnosed himself as having cancer in the stomach and he too departed for the great locoshed in the sky.

Talking of special trains being mustered at short notice reminds me of the occasion when Geoffrey Allen had the bright idea that we should go to Burton-on-Trent to have a look at the Bass/Worthington Brewery railways which were both operated by steam, the Worthington engines being green and the Bass blue, although, of course, Bass and Worthington were part of the same company. We met the public relations man who told us he had laid on the directors' saloon and complete with blue Bass loco we set off. Five minutes later we arrived at Sampling Room No 1 where a consignment of Export Bass for Belgium was available for inspection: cheerfully we re-embarked on the Special for the journey to Sampling Room No 2 where some other delectable brew was on offer. Neither of us remember very much more of what happened that day, I presume we got out of the train somewhere and somehow. I know we were taken out for lunch but I do not think that either of us could have written a word about this wonderful little railway system other than to recommend it highly to all and sundry — except CJA who would not have approved.

GFA and I had a love/hate relationship for 25 years during which time he ascended from new boy to MD of our publishing company via various editorships. Perhaps we were a little jealous of each other, he was and is an intellectual, a brilliant writer, musician, artist, in fact all the things I am not and instead of my swashbuckling commercial bent melding with his to make a solid team, the magnetic forces often repelled rather than attracted each other, which was a pity. GFA did so much for the embryonic company and he eventually decided to go it alone and become a freelance. He has done extremely well and his name is often seen not only in *Modern Railways* but in the *Daily Telegraph* and other distinguished places and he is, of course, editor of Jane's *All the World's Railways*. John W. R. Taylor, another famous author who started his early commercial life with us is editor of Jane's *All the World's Aircraft*.

Charles Simpson's first action when we took over Loco Pub Co was to march me round to Millbank to meet P. C. Allen, a director of ICI and who was burgeoning as a railway nut. We had a pleasant meeting which began a relationship which lasted for years. Peter Allen followed Beeching into the ICI chair and picked up his knighthood, wrote several books for us and inaugurated an annual railway party at his Battle home where he and his wife Consuela entertained every year a wide selection of the cream of railway nuts. It was quite an honour to be included and I think I have been

*Above:*
**Guests at one of Peter Allen's railway parties: John Scholes of the then Clapham Transport Museum, Geoffrey Freeman Allen, Ian Allan, Pat Ransome-Wallis and Pat Whitehouse.**

invited each year as have some of the regular attenders including such famous names as Hamilton-Ellis (whose patron PCA was) Maxwell, Hardy, Olver, McAlpine, Skeat, Scholes, Coiley, Manisty, Morgan, Whitehouse, MacLeod, Ransome-Wallis and dozens more. Alas, Peter had a hip operation which went wrong which rather incapacitated him but still did not debar him from overseas tours always in search of railways. He has been President of the Transport Trust and lent his name to one of the buildings of the NRM at York but I shall remember him best as genial host each summer at Battle.

I have always hated dealing with authors. They always want too much money and are never satisfied with the book you produce.

One such was the great Eric Treacy. Although in fairness I must say he never worried about the money and often if there was any, he would direct that it be given to charity but he was a real stickler when it came to quality. He was never satisfied. Eventually I arranged that he came down to Shepperton every time we were going to put one of his books to bed for him to approve the running sheets. He would duly appear, terrify the lives out of our printers but go away content. We would then meet later to look at further copies and he was wont always to pronounce himself chuffed. Invariably three days later would come a sizzling letter of complaint about minute matters of reproduction, a blob here or a filled in couple of dots there. It would take weeks to placate him and then he would settle down and be happy again. In his 'Palace' at Wakefield it always tickled me to see his engine driver's oil top and a set of greasy overalls hanging in the cloakroom besides his Episcopal mitre and vestments and he always averred he preferred to wear the former.

Treacy was a great chap, again an introduction from CJA in 1946 in Vauxhall Bridge Road when we thought up a picture book — probably the first pictures-only railway book ever published — called *Steam Up* at 10s 6d and printed in photogravure, a process which has long since disappeared. Thereafter followed a whole series of super pictorial books from his camera and somewhat less so his pen. Ossie Nock was far less formidable than any of the other authors. He was super to deal with. He would quickly agree terms without a haggle and always delivered on time: we would often make up a book together with scissors and paste and he never complained about anything. He is a real publisher's dream and even does his proof-reading superbly although he is now well into his eighties. He was such a prolific writer that Cecil would always comment that he could not possibly be doing it all himself, 'obviously he has someone to devil for him.' Which was not so, I am sure.

Contrariwise George Dow whom I first contacted in 1944 and with whom I spent many happy days later was the world's worst author to deal with. He was unsatisfiable, pernickety, difficult, aggressive but in the end forced you to do a good job with no short cuts. When he was Divisional Manager at Stoke he invited me to spend a day with him on the Cambrian line and these were the days when senior railwaymen did more or less as they pleased without counting the cost — actually I think they still do, having seen Bob Reid arrive at Kidderminster in a special train composed of one coach and a vast locomotive with only himself and small entourage on board — we had the inspection saloon and a locomotive and reasonably impressive 'hospitality' en route. To justify the expense, the Mayor of Aberystwyth was entertained to lunch on board on arrival at the town as a public relations exercise and I always envied General Managers, Divisional Managers and Engineers on their facility to whistle up their respective saloons and accompanying locomotives and go off on jaunts which would have cost the public a fortune. But why pick out the railways. Most captains of industry do things like this — in their hospitality tents. George Dow had a superb model railway in his garden 'house' at Audlem and will long be remembered for his great contribution to railway and model railway history. Dow's running mate had been Derek Barrie whom I first knew as PRO at Euston whilst Dow was at Liverpool Street. I did not particularly like him. I thought he was supercilious and pompous but he became more friendly in later years when he was appointed PRO to the British Transport Commission but I always felt he was slightly hostile. He certainly tried to put me in my place in print once or twice when I had kicked over the traces probably spurred on by John Elliot, the Chairman of the BTC, who himself once wrote me a stern letter threatening the withdrawal of all 'facilities' if I made any more public criticisms of BTC affairs.

But no-one can deny that Barry was a wonderful story-teller and his after dinner tales of exploits on railways in the Welsh valleys were apocryphal. He ultimately became GM of the Eastern Region at York which was rather surprising as he was always so much an LM man: a queer quirk too that he outran Dow, essentially an LNER man who only made it to Divisional Manager in the LM Region before retiring.

Peter Parker is a nice chap, how good a Chairman of BRB he was, I know not but he certainly was brilliant at staff and public relations: it seemed that once anyone had met him, his memory locked in and he thereafter not only remembered people by name but quite a lot about them too. He came down to Dart Valley on one occasion to have a look round and to name *Goliath* the large 2-8-0T which had just come on stream. He met me with a piece of paper in his hand and his opening gambit was, 'You are going to ask me if you can get your train into Totnes and I'm afraid you cannot.' A few months later out of the blue came a signal from Swindon inviting us to do just that and £40,000 later, the cost of a new signalling system, I signed the running powers agreement with the WR Deputy GM, Paul Witter, in

# BRITISH RAILWAYS
## THE RAILWAY EXECUTIVE

JOHN ELLIOT

*Telephone*
PADDINGTON 1601

A.

CHAIRMAN'S ROOM
222, MARYLEBONE ROAD
LONDON, N.W. 1

PERSONAL.

30th August, 1951.

*My dear Allan.*

      I am obliged to you for sending me the really beautiful book on the "Bulleid Pacifics," and as one who had something to do with the introduction of these locomotives from a policy point of view when I was Deputy General Manager of the Southern Railway, I am glad to see that you have given them such a fine tribute.    They had their teething troubles, and their permanent ones, too, but they gave us *(S.R)* the best motive power we ever had and had a good deal to do with the remarkable improvement in timekeeping.

      Mr. Bulleid has a highly original and inventive mind, and his name will live in locomotive history.

      I am glad to see that you go from success to success.    I remember your early days at Waterloo and the difficulties that had to be overcome.

      I read a letter from you in the "Railway Gazette" a little time ago, and while, no doubt, it was meant to be light and humorous, particularly the first paragraph, in fact I thought it was facetious and not in the best of taste, seeing that the previous Companies, and now British Railways, have helped you considerably.    Constructive criticism is good for us, but I am sure your father would agree with me that you are not really ideally placed to have a free hand in these matters, having regard to the close connection between our two organisations.    You can't have it both ways!

*With every good wish.*

Yours sincerely,

Ian Allan, Esq.,
282, Vauxhall Bridge Road,
Westminster,
London, S.W.1.

*John Elliot*

the pouring rain and the first train went in. It was an economic mini-disaster and we wished BR had stuck to PP's guns.

But during that visit he never missed a trick, putting his head into every nook and cranny to say hello to anyone who might feel forgotten and as he stepped forward to unveil the engine nameplate he spotted the Bishop of Exeter nearby. 'This is a job for you Bishop,' he shouted, to which the Bishop replied, 'No, you christen it, I'll confirm it.'

Nobody contributed more to the firm in political and financial terms than Willie Brett and later Norman Miles but one chap who really ran the show for 20 years was Jack. In 1952 I needed a gardener and Jack appeared on his bike for interview. I recognised him immediately as a policeman regularly on point duty in Staines, now retired after 25 years in the force. We clicked immediately and he signed on for one day a week: he was as strong as a horse and I would say with rather more brawn than brain but a super chap in every way. We got stuck for packing at the office and I asked him to give us a hand. Very quickly one day a week became two, then three and eventually seven. He reported every day of the year except for 10 days when he went on holiday. He even appeared on Christmas morning to make sure we were all right, to clean the shoes, clean the boiler, sweep up the leaves. He was a gem. Once the children arrived he was a first-rate nursemaid and he and his wife were babysitters when needed. He was never ill, would resign in a huff about eight times a year but never left us until his terminal illness at the age of 82. He was the power behind the packing department which, of course, was the last link in the publishing production chain. Effectively, therefore, he knew exactly what was happening in every department and when and why there were problems and delays. He used to come with me each day in the car to the office and return with me in the evening. I was regaled by innumerable stories of life in the Metropolitan Police (mostly of violence, mild bribery and corruption) between 1927 and 1952 and his philosophy of life in the mornings and the shortcomings of everyone in the company in the evenings always premising his remarks by, 'Don't say I told you,' and finishing, 'I haven't told you anything but just go and look at so and so and find out for yourself.' He then gave me the clues and I had to sort out the problems next day with him standing innocently

*Above right:*
**The naming of Dart Valley 2-8-0T *Goliath* by Peter Parker.**

*Right:*
**Signing the running powers agreement between the Dart Valley Light Railway plc and British Rail in a rainstorm just outside Totnes. Ian Allan and Paul Witter (Deputy General Manager, Western Region) exchange contracts and the inaugural train is permitted on to the hallowed territory of British Rail.**

*Above:*
**Staff relations: Charles and Freda Hemmings with Kenn and Muriel Groves supervised by Jack Deller.**

by with the expression of having no idea what all the fuss was about. At the age of 82 he was still working and a good six-footer and one evening on his regular stroll to the pub for a nightcap at about 10pm, two youths approached him; one roughly knocked his hat off saying, 'Wotcher grandpa'. Jack grabbed aforesaid youth by the tie with his left hand whilst the other delivered a straight right which laid the yob flat on his back; he was yanked up again by his tie and told, 'Don't you ever do that again,' and as the louts turned and fled, the other one felt his boot on his backside.

And the last of the personalities I shall include is Bernard Whitehall — or Bernie the Bolt as he was generally known. I first met him just before he was appointed (the last) Divisional Manager of the South Western Division of BR — *my* division since my wartime days at Waterloo — so I was delighted when he came to Wimbledon. A non-stop talker who burst with enthusiasm for all the great ideas he had and a person who had so much confidence in himself that I think he really believed nothing could possibly go awry and by and large, the SW Division did well under him. Perhaps he did not influence me as I had grown old by the time he came on the scene but he gave me a few laughs of which I recount two. He wanted to try and speed up the Portsmouth service and decided to run a trial using 4-REP units off the Bournemouth line which were more powerful than the 4-CIG units usually employed on the Portsmouth fast service. He invited me to come with him: there were a handful of his chaps and that was all. The line was to be clear and nothing could go wrong - he said. We left Waterloo in fine style, hit our first 'yellow' just after Vauxhall and proceeded to crawl from yellow to yellow all the way to Hampton Court junction where we got our first 'green'. The offending train which had been holding us up all the way from Clapham Junction which had then switched to the slow line turned out to be no less than a light engine propelling *his* inspection saloon on a crew training, route learning jaunt. Of course, the whole object of his train timing special was lost as we were now at least 10 minutes behind schedule and our 'path' lost. He was very cross and showed it.

Some time later we decided to do a rerun of the 'Atlantic Coast Express' from Waterloo to Torrington. 'Nothing,' said Bernie the Bolt again, 'can possibly go wrong', at any rate as far as Sherborne where he handed over to the Western Region. He turned out an immaculate train. It really was beautiful and we bowled along in great style almost to Sherborne when we drew to a dead stop with a very severe brake application. We all looked out to find that we had gone half a train length past a red signal. The guard got out: the signal cleared and in his excitement to get the train away, Bernard shouted to the driver to go which he did but the guard did not and was left standing aghast on the ballast. It poured with rain all the way there and all the way back but it was a super day out and, alas, the South Western Division went the way of all flesh and we can all see what happens now when you try to run an intensive service like the Southern without adequate hands-on management.

*Above:*
**'Atlantic Coast Express' rerun at Barnstaple. Bernard Whitehall's immaculate train with special personalised headcode.** *Colin J. Marsden*

# 14

# Preservation Scene

In 1968 Pat Whitehouse had started being nice to me and I wondered what he wanted. He and Birmingham accountant Pat Garland had become involved, he said, with some Devon folk who were trying to acquire and preserve the Totnes and Ashburton branch and had not a clue as to how to do it. Would I like to join the Board — subject to an investment of a few thousand pounds. I agreed and was invited to a meeting at Bristol at which I was elected. On the Board were the local big shots, Brigadier Sir Ralph Rayner DL, Peter Sutcliffe, the boss of Dartington Hall, John Evans, a Torquay architect, Plymouth surveyor Peter Steadman, Bob Saunders CEng and the two Pats. This and subsequent meetings started about 11am and went on and on to 4pm and after; there appeared to be no chairman and in my naivety I commented on this suggesting that as PBW was, in fact, chairing the meetings, we made it official which was agreed.

The track was still in situ and the former stationmaster at Buckfastleigh, Dick Dinwiddy, still in his house there. He acted as guide and watchdog over the premises and locos puffed around from time to time. Our Bristol meetings gradually began to fructify though it seemed we were not going to be likely to get any trains to Ashburton as the A38 modernisation was planned to enfold the track bed. Our fears proved correct, the M-o-T would not grant a light railway order for the Buckfastleigh-Ashburton section and despite an expensive appeal, the day was lost and the A38 began to obliterate the attractive rail route to Ashburton and its Brunel-roofed station.

However, the LRO for the Buckfastleigh-Totnes section did come forth though access into Totnes was denied. The great day for the opening arrived in 1972. PBW asked me to take over the publicity arrangements. Dr Beeching was invited to come and open the line he had so recently closed and had agreed to do so; the Buckfastleigh site went *en fête* and the directors and their wives all dressed in their Sunday best mounted the rostrum for this splendid occasion before resorting to the beer tent where a splendid spread had been laid on, and all very reminiscent of what must have happened at the original openings of railways a hundred years earlier. After the photocalls and other fripperies had taken place, Dr Beeching departed and our beloved leader suddenly realised that he had invited the Bishop of Exeter but had not yet made use of his services and felt it prudent to ask

*Above:*
**Ian Allan Ltd ran the first railway bookshop for the Dart Valley Railway in the former goods shed at Buckfastleigh.**

him to invoke a blessing on the railway, then deputed me to lay it on. The Bishop was amenable but where on earth could I organise an episcopal blessing on a railway site? The Treacy precedent of using a loco tender to deliver a sermon had not by then been created — the beer tent was the only answer so the assembled directors were shepherded into the unhallowed hall of Bacchus and the Bishop not only blessed the railway but prayed for the Company's commercial success. A prayer which has been duly answered.

I cannot tell too much of the progress of our Board meetings as the information must be privileged and as many of the protagonists are still alive, I would fear for the libel actions which might follow. Suffice it to say, it was all usually good fun. Ralph Rayner was a typical 'county' squire and spoke with such a plum in his mouth that he was totally incomprehensible but never finished a sentence anyway. His director's file was identified by a postcard of Thomas the Tank engine with wobbly eyes stuck to it and his only contribution was to bring mulled wine to meetings in the winter and champagne in the summer, something of which I did not really approve. John Evans used to fawn over him addressing him always with a deferential 'Sir' and appropriate grovel and the Brigadier always referred to me as the 'stormy petrel from London'. As each chairman did his stint there would be a brief conspiracy to depose him after a year or so and when it came to Peter Sutcliffe's turn to be deposed he appointed me in his stead in 1976. I survived as long as he did and when he died 10 years later I received a report that the expected conspiracy had been held in the Waterman's Arms at Buckfastleigh where the next chairman was nominated and subsequently appointed: he was sensible, did three years, remarried and withdrew bloodlessly and John Evans took over in 1990 and much to my surprise is making an excellent job of it.

During the years from 1972 so much happened. Bill Faulkner had been recruited as General Manager from the Talyllyn Railway but he did not like Devon and returned to Wales after one season. I realised that Terry Holder, now retired from *The Economist*, was available and approached him, the Pats interviewed him and he became MD. With his enormous flair and enthusiasm he soon had the show humming though as a salesman he never knew the difference between turnover and profit. We took a lot of money but did not make a lot of profit but what he did do was to see the tremendous potential of the about to be closed line from Paignton to Kingswear and its connection to Dartmouth; he also saw the danger to the Dart Valley line if a competitor got his hands on this superb coastal link between Torbay and Dartmouth.

The whole line and most of Kingswear waterfront was acquired for £0.25m and the company went public. That was disaster No 1. Disaster No 2 was to sell off all the surplus land thus acquired to recover the £0.25m. Had DVLR retained the frontage at Kingswear and the land at Goodrington a little longer, the company would have made a killing. But it all seemed right at the time and jobbing backwards gets no parsnips buttered.

Terry Holder recruited an understudy, Barry Cogar, a supermarket manager from far off Tavistock who was a keen volunteer but he was deemed too young to take over when Terry departed and a succession of managers and chairmen followed over whom and their activities we draw a veil. Eventually the great light dawned and Barry Cogar was appointed General Manager and has remained so ever since and also became a director.

There were thrills and spills during my reign. Romney Hythe & Dymchurch

*Above:*
**Dart Valley friends at Churston: Barry Cogar (General Manager), Rob Woodman, Ken Woodruff (Mid Hants), Chris Peyton and John Evans.**

141

were having problems in Kent which had been deserted by tourists and were casting around for a new site. Their GM, John Snell, cast his eyes on the Torbay line as being ideal for a 15in gauge railway and presented a very elaborate plan for removing the standard gauge track and replacing it with a double track 15in gauge system. It could have been a wow but it was felt that 15in gauge just could not carry the traffic and the idea was turned down. It was, however, thought that a 15in gauge line from Buckfastleigh to Totnes might breathe new life into this commercially ailing railway. As soon as news of this suggestion reached the ears of the Dart Valley Railway Association, the membership went berserk and it was quite impossible to convince them that no decisions had been taken, it was merely an idea that we should look at. They continued to rage and shout abuses at the Company — as was and is their wont — and in the end Romney's survey showed the project was impossible anyway and they withdrew.

As a plc with publicly quoted shares, there was always the danger of a takeover and when the Board discovered that 'Ron the Raider' Brierly was acquiring DVLR plc shares, they naturally pricked up their ears and bore in mind the valuable freehold estate the Company owned at Buckfastleigh, Staverton, Kingswear and Paignton. It was necessary to assess the value of the land to an asset stripper and let the shareholders know what their holding was worth. To try to prove this the Company put in an outline planning application to shorten the line a hundred or so yards north of the present station at Kingswear and build flats on the riverside frontage. All hell was let loose. Residents and railway nuts joined in the abuse at such a dastardly plan. The local authority slapped a 'listing' order on Kingswear station, described then as being held together by the woodworms joining hands. Came the AGM and the fur really flew. Hard as I tried to explain that we had no intention of carrying out the plan, which was merely to find out the planning potential and, therefore, value of the site, the shareholders refused to believe us and I think that was one of the few times I have ever got really rattled in a public debate or as Garland described it, 'I noticed you suddenly moved into overdrive.' I remember returning home on the train that evening with Chris Peyton our financial director and Pat Garland when we were all so fed up with our shareholders, we knocked back three double gin and tonics between Newton Abbot and Taunton and charged them to the Company.

Which was all quite daft as the planners turned the application down flat and that was that. It did alert the shareholders and the public to likely predators and eventually Ron Brierly sold his shareholding and disappeared from the Dart Valley scene.

On departing from the chair of Dart Valley but still remaining an active director, I was encouraged to move to the chair of the Association of Minor

Railways, the trade link-up of all the preserved railways. This had been formed before World War 2 and had been regurgitated in 1970 but had not really established itself as a viable force. The appointment was to me an honour and a challenge. We changed the name to Association of Independent Railways and turned it into a company limited by guarantee and hope we have sharpened up its purpose and performance; certainly we bring together all the crowned heads of the railway preservation movement at least twice a year. My involvement has brought me into close touch with the directors and general managers of all the independent railways and I find it both enjoyable and edifying and I hope our membership which comprises almost every publicly operated railway feels the same. If nothing else, I introduced a Rail Pass scheme whereby every railwayist on one independent railway could ride freely on that of every other participating company.

The Ian Allan Group's involvement in railways at home and, indeed, all over the world is quite considerable as our periodicals touch on all railway matters. One particular involvement is with AIR's stable mate, the Association of Railway Preservation Societies (ARPS) with whom annually is staged a competition for the best preserved station or railway structure. We work with BR and the National Coal Board (who naturally have a commercial interest in coal-burning railways) who also subsidise the event. The judgement culminates in a presentation of awards ranging from beautiful and chiselled slate plaques to rather mundane certificates presented by such notables as Prince Michael of Kent, the Lord Mayor of London and various BRB chairmen.

Our close association, therefore, with ARPS, AIR and the preservation movement generally, is one we value though it seems to cost us a lot of money in subsidies, hidden and overt. Still, it's nice to be given a footplate ride every now and again.

# 15

# Organics and Motors

Enough of the fun and games of independent railways and back to the hard graft of running a business for prior to all this the Rotary connection had raised its head again. Ron Silver was a leading member of Shepperton Rotary and next door neighbour of Kenn Groves. His Rotary classification was 'Fertiliser distributor', something which caused no little ribald comment from time to time. He ran a firm called Chase Organics (Great Britain) Ltd which specialised in the production and sale of seaweed products worldwide. The principal shareholder was Jocelyn Chase who had inherited the business and a lot of land in the Chertsey/Shepperton area from his father; he had been a naughty boy and got out of the country fairly sharpish with the police on his tail and settled in Argentina. He left the management of the company entirely to Ron Silver but sent him weekly instructions close typed on flimsy paper running into several pages. He also despatched himself on worldwide 'selling' tours and sending in very few orders but quite large expense claims. Although Chase owned the business and in effect was free to do what he like with it, Ron Silver was not the sort of chap to stomach that; he was trying to run a successful business and deeply resented the intrusions from Argentina. Eventually the storm broke and he notified Chase that one of them had to go, surprisingly Chase agreed on condition that someone he considered reliable was appointed in his place. For some reason Silver nominated me and even more surprisingly Chase accepted me. I hope Ron does not think it was the worst day's work he ever did but he could not be blamed if he did so think as I was unwittingly eventually to be responsible for his losing his interest in the company.

Chase turned his closely typed flimsy missives on me. As his agent I felt bound to try to deal with them but he was so out of touch and over the top in his proposals that I found myself eventually sending back a few platitudes to keep him quiet using all the technical terms like kelp and cytokynins to try to impress him with my subject knowledge. It did not quite work for he must have felt that sufficient water had flowed under sufficient bridges for him to make sorties to England without too much risk of his past misdemeanours catching up with him and he notified us one day that he was coming to the AGM. Not only did he come but he proposed and by demanding a poll and using his majority shareholding carried a vote of no confidence in MD Silver. Silver refused to resign, Chase refused to sack

*Above:*
**The first venture into the motor business. Allan Chase Motors at Wentworth.**

him. The chairman and only other director, Michael Ransom, was non-plussed. I said I did not want to be a director of a company without a reliable MD and withdrew my nomination for re-election and went back to my own office for tea. Eventually the meeting broke up in disorder. Silver went home and stayed there and Chase Organics had an 85 year-old to run it pending his return to Argentina in a few weeks' time.

After a week of stalemate, it seemed ridiculous to let a good company and all its staff just go down the drain and anyway, as a director, I had put in a lot of hard work not least of all causing with Ron a new freehold headquarters building to be constructed and occupied. Norman Miles and I got hold of Chase and suggested that Ian Allan Group should purchase the shares and effect a take-over. Chase had given a lot of shares away to his mates over the years and it was quite a picnic finding all the shareholders and getting them to accept our bid. Meanwhile, Chase had agreed with Silver to pay his full salary until his official retirement, a commitment we took over eventually. It was a sorry tale. Chase went back to Argentina and returned eventually to England where he died at Happisborough whilst Ron Silver, who did not feel inclined to become an employee of Ian Allan Group, quietly withdrew though I am glad to say we have remained close friends ever since and we play cards together every month.

Before the Chase saga blew its top, the Rotary connection rotated again into our direction. Doug Skeggs was the local motor trader and Ford garage proprietor in Shepperton. He had a good site in the middle of the High Street and had a super business which he and his wife ran together. We had been friends for some time and we had even taken our respective wives and children on holiday together in France. He was the same age within three weeks as I and shared a lot of common ideas; we were both very keen on business and as the two larger concerns in Shepperton, vied with each other even to the extent of having rival football teams playing matches which he always won though I never realised at the time that half his players were imported heavies who made mincemeat of our lightweight printers, publishers and travel agents.

Skeggs grew his business hard. He took on Volvo at a site in Virginia Water; opened a branch at Ashford then Esher and eventually Shoreham. In fact, he ran before he could walk and on one fateful 1 August he came into our office near to tears; the Midland Bank had at 11.30am given him two hours to repay his overdraft, something he had no hope of doing and the Bank had picked the very day in the year when the Skeggs' account would be at its richest with the annual rush of new car sales. By 2pm the Receiver was in. Could we help?

Norman Miles and I asked why on earth he had not come sooner as once the Receiver was in everything was in his hands. 'Try,' he said, 'to recover Virginia Water — that's the best of the bunch.' Ron Silver was also a mate of Skeggs and Chase were looking for somewhere to invest their reserves and so we decided to go in jointly as Chase and Ian Allan and eventually emerged as Allan Chase Motors though not for long. Norman saw the Receiver and did the deal. We bought Skeggs' garage at Virginia Water on the basis that Doug Skeggs would run it on our behalf and thereby keep himself employed and give us a new interest. The Receiver would not let us have any of the rest of the Skeggs empire which he quickly disposed of elsewhere.

In the event Doug was offered a deal with the chap who bought the Shepperton site and decided not to come with us to Virginia Water but offered his son and wife instead. We gladly took them on board as we had no knowledge whatsoever or experience of the motor business. Fate struck another blow. Volvo was unhappy with the Skeggs connection and threatened to withdraw the franchise. There was no hassle, the Skeggs realised our predicament and withdrew.

And there we were, Ron Silver and our lot, alone with a garage business, petrol pumps, showrooms and no-one to run the show. We put in our internal auditor, John Nicol, and told him to get on with it which he did with great success. The Chase blow-up then occurred and with Ian Allan Group's acquisition of the Chase shares, we fell heir to the share of Allan Chase Motors Ltd and soon changed the name to Ian Allan Motors Ltd.

So another entirely accidental and serendipitous entry into an entirely new line of business. We had become fertilizer distributors and garage proprietors overnight.

# 16

# A Few Other Activities

When you have run your own business for years it is difficult to assess whether you are really any good at anything in other people's eyes so it was with some surprise and pleasure that on the retirement of our Lodge Secretary I was appointed into the job and it was even more surprising when the following year I landed up as Secretary of the Amicable Society of Blues. This is a very ancient dining society. In fact it claims to be the oldest in London if not the world, having started eating in 1629 and been at it ever since. It meets thrice yearly and is formed of distinguished alumni of Christ's Hospital, governors or officers in one of the City Livery Halls.

There is nothing very unusual about organising the odd dinner and the great thing is that you can choose the menu and always decide that everyone is going to eat and drink what the Secretary likes. Writing the minutes is a different cup of tea. The 'Amicables', who have included Charles Lamb, Barnes Wallis, Ian Trethowan and a string of other names I could drop, are an odd lot and 'brawl' throughout the evening for which fines are levied from the chair and trying to set a record down in a fairly humorous and interesting way is not the easiest of tasks though I have now done it for 20 years and enjoy the utter power that the office enjoys, for Presidents come and Presidents go annually but Secretaries go on for ever.

I rather suspect that my involvement with the Amicables led me to a close association with the royal hospitals and the City of London. In 1975 an interesting thing happened. Mollie and I went, as has been my wont from time immemorial, to Speech Day at Christ's Hospital and at lunch I sat next to John Hansford, the Head Master of King Edward's School, Witley, the offshoot of Bridewell Royal Hospital which with Christ's Hospital, St Thomas' Bethlehem and Bart's was one of the five Royal hospitals founded in 1553 by King Edward VI. Three things were curious, firstly that my father had been a governor of Bridewell and Bethlehem, secondly John Hansford and I had been to the same prep school, Homefield at Sutton, at the same time and that my father had been instrumental in getting him a place at Christ's Hospital when his father had died suddenly; the third curiosity was that the Sanatorium Sister at King Edward's School was the daughter of our vicar at Laleham, also an Old Blue as the alumni of CH are known.

Hansford invited us to visit King Edward's School at Witley and we duly turned up, were given a tour of the impressive school buildings and entertained to lunch on the high table. To my surprise and amazement, some weeks later I had a letter from the Treasurer, their pet word for Chairman of the Governors, the Earl of Selborne, inviting me to become a school governor. Needless to say I was very chuffed and accepted with great pleasure. I duly turned up as a very new boy and sat quietly through the first few meetings. John Selborne was an excellent chairman despite being the third Earl, the line having been started by a Lord Chancellor in the early 19th century. The meetings were extremely formal and composed largely of aldermen and common councilmen of the City of London to whose charge Edward VI delivered the Foundation all those years ago. Nobody said anything very positive, the leads came always from the chair and no matter what anyone suggested, a smiling and polite response let it be known that everything was already buttoned up. I thoroughly enjoyed working with Selborne who did a tremendous amount for the Foundation which was just beginning to recover from a financial crisis which had caused it to sell most of its property, pictures and silver. He steered the ship very wisely through those difficult years and I and some of the others who managed to break the bonds of formality started to get more involved with the operation of the school and began to humanise the meetings.

In 1980 the Treasurer of Christ's Hospital approached me and invited me to join the Council of Almoners, the inner governing body of CH and described to me by a leading member, Prof Jack Morpurgo, as being 'merely an extension of the "Amicables" '. This was a great honour, perhaps the highest that CH could bestow on any of its friends. And back I found myself in the Court Room at Great Tower Street where all those years ago we had formulated the first edition of *Trains Illustrated*. CH Council Meetings were awful and awe-ful and I hated them. The accoustics in the Court Room were impossible and roving microphones were provided, though by the time one had acquired one, and in the prevailing pompous atmosphere, one had virtually forgotten what was in mind when the time came to say it. I did react to one or two odd financial decisions and was immediately drafted on to the Finance Committee which was certainly more interesting, though I found my somewhat verbose colleagues though lovable a bit tiresome. My patience was often sorely tried and I could never understand why the various chairmen never shut them up. There were intrigues of all sorts and so much information which should have been available to us was not, heads rolled or perhaps I should say Heads. It was exciting but time consuming and I was back to my roots.

Then one evening in 1982 as I lay half asleep on the floor looking at some boring tv programme the phone rang; it was John Selborne who had some time before intimated that after 11 years he proposed to depart from the chair of KES. He asked me whether I had considered who his successor should be and I mentioned a few likely names, when to my surprise he said. 'No — it's you.' I was a bit nonplussed but he was reassuring, 'It's only five meetings a year and you read a lesson at the Carol Service.'

I said I would consider the matter. Two days later the Earl rang again and I accepted, subject, of course, to election by the 25 Aldermen and goodness knows how many common councilmen of the City of London. Amazingly they agreed and in 1983 I was 'sworn in' at Guildhall.

Being a fairly senior member of the CH fraternity and Treasurer of Bridewell as well as an active director of Dart Valley, Sunday engine driver on the Great Cockcrow Railway and several other local affairs and running our own Group, kept me reasonably busy and I soon discovered the falsehood of John Selborne's brief.

After taking over the reins of Chairman at Witley, life was quiet for a few weeks then one morning at 6am the 'phone rang. It was the Head Master. 'Have you heard the news on the radio?' I said, 'No' and pointed out that as it was only 6am it was unlikely that I would have. 'Well,' he said, 'when you do, you will hear that a party of children have been lost in a snowstorm on the Cairngorms — and they are ours.' No more sleep for me as I tossed and

*Above:*
**From time to time we have VIP visits to Shepperton; here Graham Leonard, then Bishop of London, has Uncle Mac showing off his library.**

turned at the awful prospect of dealing with distraught parents. Mercifully by the 7am news the party had been found and were safe but without much credit to their guides and, therefore, the School. That night the *Evening Standard* blared its criticism across its whole front page.

Later on another early morning call. The Sanatorium Sister had been attacked during the night by an intruder who had held her at knifepoint for hours on end. On another occasion when we were out with friends enjoying a quiet game of cards one evening, the 'phone rang. It was the Bursar to say that the school was on fire, there had been a complete evacuation and fire brigades were on the way. So much for that 'five meetings a year and you read the lesson at the Carol Service.'

These were just a few of the alarms and excursions and I can tell you that being Chairman of a 525-strong boarding school is no sinecure. So much so that by 1989 I felt I couldn't do justice to both CH and KES and regretfully on the completion of my term of office and after 10 years did not offer myself for re-election to the CH council. The task at King Edward's continues. We still have a large collection of 150-year old buildings to be modernised and the Children Act and multitudinous other Government regulations to cope with. I am on my fourth Head teacher, 10th visit by a Lord Mayor in office who turns up in state for every Speech Day and second visit of our President, Queen Elizabeth the Queen Mother who really makes our day on visits and always shows great interest in our affairs. I quite enjoy mixing with the city nobs and surprisingly even met Bob Reid I at Christ's Hospital one day as Master of the Carmen's Company. Strange is it not how we all live double lives!

I mentioned earlier one latter-day rail excursion that ended in utter disaster; well, actually it did not end in disaster, it was a disaster from the start. We wanted something special to commemorate our 40th Anniversary in 1982 so I contacted Sir Peter Parker, the British Railways Board Chairman, and asked him to bless what we hoped might be the longest non-stop run ever attempted, Paddington-Bristol-Leeds-Carlisle-Edinburgh and back direct by East Coast main line to King's Cross. Sir Peter quite enthusiastically agreed and passed the arrangements down the line. An HST unit with full kitchen facilities was allocated from the Eastern Region, costings agreed and the trip advertised. It was an immediate sell-out at £35 a time which was quite a lot in those days. The train complete with 'Ian Allan' headboard duly arrived at Paddington and set off non-stop for Edinburgh. At Reading, a stray passenger for Taunton realised he was going off course and appealed to the guard for help; the guard not realising the significance of his action, caused the train to stop at Tilehurst to unload aforesaid passenger and lost two or three valuable minutes, causing the 'non-stop' to lose its path and stop again just outside Bristol to let an HST service train

*Above:*
**Company hostesses pose before the ill-fated 'Ian Allan Limited' at Newcastle.**

through at Dr Day's junction. The non-stop then proceeded to the former LMS line and stopped at the first signal for 15 minutes before the driver discovered it was u/s. Now nearly 20 minutes late, the train fouled up through the Birmingham area and was over 60 minutes late by Sheffield where the restaurant car crew demanded a platform stop to fill up their depleted water tanks. Away from Sheffield the train ran into an ambush of vandals who hurled bricks at the train breaking two of the double glazed windows. That, said two off-duty CME chaps who were riding the train for fun — and proving invaluable allies — puts an end to high speed running until the windows are replaced though it was doubtful whether this could be done in Edinburgh in one hour on a Saturday afternoon.

We eventually arrived at Carlisle and whilst we were having urgent talks on the platform as to whether to go on to Edinburgh and chance it, notwithstanding that London Transport were going on strike at 10.30 that night, or take a short cut across to Newcastle, the decision had been made for us, the signal at the south end of the platform cleared, the new guard blew his whistle and Edinburgh was abandoned. Two hours were now available to explore the Newcastle Metro whilst the windows were repaired and as the train was about to make a punctual departure, alarms sounded, an ambulance roared on to the platform and one of the passengers was carried off with a suspected heart attack. More delay and frustration but no matter, a message was flashed through that the signalbox at Selby had been struck by lightning and all services were to be diverted. We had the distinct feeling that 'someone up there' had it in for us that day. Fortunately by the time the alleged non-stop had reached York and everyone abandoned themselves to fate, the mess at Selby had been overcome and the train did, in fact, get back to King's Cross just in time to beat the LT stoppage.

After a lot of argument, BR agreed to allow all the passengers a free ride to Edinburgh and back on a service train but it took a lot more argument and insistence that they got first class and not second class tickets. But they did. Despite the succession of hogsnortons as Fiennes would have described it, most of the passengers enjoyed the fiasco almost entirely as a moment by moment commentary and explanation of the disasters from John Huntley and Peter Semmens was relayed by the train's intercom. The whole story even made *Private Eye*.

Things have an annoying habit sometimes of going wrong at the wrong times. It happened to us twice. One morning very shortly after Christmas, we were having a Board meeting when the report was rushed to us that there had been a bomb explosion in our travel shop at Brentford and several of our staff had been injured. The shop had just been completely refurbished with new carpets, ceilings, furniture — the lot. Fortunately there was little personal damage, a few cuts and bruises, but naturally quite a shocked staff. The shop was in ruins. We later found out that it was not a bomb at all; there had been a gas leak next door which had obviously leaked all over the Christmas holiday and the proverbial 'first footer' that came in and provided any form of ignition blew the place up. Of course, the insurance company covered the damage but why oh why could we not have blown up before we did our original refurbishment: it would have been much more economic.

We did the same at Terminal House and completely renovated our reception area at very considerable expense. One night about 10.30pm I was stretched out, as is my wont you will have gathered, on the floor half asleep with one eye on a tv football match, when the 'phone rang. It was Alf Pitfield.

'Your office is on fire, I think you'd better come and see it.' I checked somewhat incredulously to see whether it was 1 April but he sounded serious and I leapt into the car. On arrival at Shepperton five minutes later I found half a dozen fire engines, police and the faithful Kenn Groves who had got there before me. The place was devastated and the smoke had permeated everywhere. The walls were black 100 yards from the seat of the blaze. The firemen were jolly good and did their best but in the end we were left with a gigantic mess to clear up which ultimately cost £93,000 to rectify. Again, insurance covered the amount but what a pity the lunatics who put the bit

*Above:*
**The reception hall in Terminal House after the fire.**

*Below:*
**Crash! The day a British Rail train failed to stop at Shepperton station. It provided good publicity for Ian Allan Travel as it straddled their offices and made headlines in the national press.**

*Above:*
**Opening the new station st Shepperton with Stan Smith, the local Area Manager.**

of burning rag through the letter box had not done it a few weeks earlier before we had spent our own good money on the job.

The travel company had grown, no longer was it a shoe string operation, it was very slick and had divided itself into retail and business house sectors all with the very latest in technology and with an elaborate corporate image of shop fronts, staff uniforms and interior decor. It employed 250 staff and became the senior partner in the organisation.

As our two boys grew up in the business, it was seen to fall naturally into two divisions 'graphics' and 'leisure' orientated. David having had an upbringing in books and magazines automatically gravitated towards graphics whilst Paul with his wide experience of stamping travel brochures turned to 'leisure' — travel, motors and the hotel of which companies each ultimately became respectively chairmen.

The property holding company, Ian Allan Developments Ltd, became Tennay Properties Ltd — as there were ten 'As' — Mollie and I, David and Gillian, Paul and Jane and four grandchildren, we should have waited for it would have become Twelveay quite soon afterwards.

The Motor company was thriving at Virginia Water with its Volvo franchise despite the fact that it was well away from Staines which was the hub of the franchise area and Volvo were becoming restive that we were not in the right place. Just as we had sought hotels, so now were we hunting for garage premises but without much luck for sites were few and far between and in great demand; the prospect of getting planning consent for new sites was absolutely zilch. Then, suddenly, David Larmuth, our motoring supremo got wind through the grapevine of a good site then currently the local Daimler/Jaguar dealer, that he wanted out and quickly. Fortunately we were in a position and under pressure to move quickly and in we went to good main road frontage on the old A30 immediately between Staines and Egham.

Volvo were pleased and so were we; in fact, Volvo were so pleased they pointed us in the direction of Wimbledon where the Volvo dealer was wanting to move on. Again, after a brief horsetrade we acquired his showroom premises in Kingston Road, South Wimbledon and his workshop at Prince George's Road, Merton. A split site is not ideal but not unusual and with our home grown team from Staines and Virginia Water, we were able to set up a very viable operation.

Meanwhile, Virginia Water took on board the Land Rover/Range Rover franchise with excellent initial results when Land Rover following Volvo's example started to make demands for bigger and better premises. After endless haggling with the planners, a design was agreed for a brand new showroom and premises and the work was miraculously carried out whilst the entire business of selling, prospecting. servicing and parts supply carried on. We then went on to acquire a small petrol station and showroom adjacent to Thorpe Park as an adjunct to the Egham/Staines operation which had become swamped with cars and business, so John Nicol's original timid start had proceeded forward until Paul and David Larmuth had between them built a two-franchise, five branch company with a multi-million pound turnover per annum and which was beginning to eclipse even the travel company's cash flow except of course that in Travel cash flows in and stays in for a time before flowing out. In Motors it flows out and out and out until you sell a few cars.

By the middle of the 1980s our Group of companies presented a very different and unpredictable face from that of the 1960s when publishing and printing were our mainstays. The Travel company with its enormous £40m turnover and tentacles stretching from Croydon to Taunton and Birmingham had predominated our activities, then one day I was invited by Hoseasons on a jolly on the River Thames and chatted as we cruised along with a chap I had known for some years and who was now in charge of W. H. Smith's Group Travel operation. He suggested that we talked about a take-over, such an unthinkable idea that I turned him down flat. Other overtures followed from other 'big boys' and I talked to Hogg Robinson to try to discover the temperature of the water or rather to see what was on offer in terms of hard cash. Then suddenly something blew up inside me and I finished up in hospital and the boys found themselves with a firm offer from W. H. Smith. I was not in favour of accepting the bid but felt too rough to argue other than to insist that our Shepperton operation of business and retail travel was omitted from the deal. Paul and Norman Miles then did the business. What a bit of luck. I was too sick to worry for obviously the right action had been taken. Travel nationwide nose-dived and later with the Gulf War and recession landed flat on its back. So much so that WHS closed a lot of the branches they had bought from us and sold back to us the business house centres at Bracknell, Windsor and Brentford for something a lot less than we sold them.

We became temporarily cash rich but not for long and in order to avoid penal capital taxation embarked on a wide ranging investment scheme which included the acquisition of a large new office block which was in course of construction on the site of Shepperton station and former goods yard. I was even asked officially to declare the new station open and unveil a plaque to say I did it. We refurbished our printing company completely and bought the freeholds of as many premises we occupied as possible. To get the benefit of the 'roll-over' of capital profit we had to move into new premises known as 'Clock House', a step I took with some reluctance as I was very happy in Terminal House with its commanding view of Shepperton High Street. But this was progress and up to the big house we moved: we decided to retain Terminal House and the address and our Retail Travel and Regalia offices remained there, the rest we let off to the local business community in small units. Thus, Tennay Properties Ltd which started off as a tiny offshoot, had become the owner of quite a few million pounds worth of real estate, none of which has ever had a charge, mortgage or any other encumbrance attached to it, which is one achievement which gives a little bit of pride even if it nearly finished off a senior bank official.

Rising costs decided us in 1991 to rethink our book and magazine distribution arrangements for the cost of employing our own staff entirely for our own products was proving totally uneconomic and, indeed, the whole publishing scene nationwide was not very healthy. We, therefore, opened two of our own retail outlets in Birmingham and London (where else?), and put our magazine and books to contractors and filled the empty space at Coombelands by transferring to these both the regalia company and Chase Organics, both of whom were expanding and needed more space. Chase had amalgamated its growing (sic) organic seed business with that of the Henry Doubleday Research Association and thereby looking to treble its turnover.

*Above:*
**Inside the Birmingham bookshop.**

The latest development in the Group's story is the recovery of Pitfield House, sub-let to engineers in 1978 who in turn assigned their sub-lease to the adjacent Station Garage as a bodyshop and paint works. The need for a crash repair shop had become a necessary adjunct to the motor company who arranged to buy the business and recover the sub-lease and at the same time purchasing the freehold from the BR Property Board. Thus Ian Allan Motors have become a complete unit, but not for long for the Paul Allan/David Larmuth set up is far too restless to stop and felt that the Volvo and Land Rover ranges were too far up the market and needed a range of small cars to meet appropriate customer needs so that when a garage at Old Woking offered itself they quickly moved in to add the Peugeot franchise to their clutch. Needless to say, complete refurbishing and a new image in the IA style was essential and the latest addition to the Ian Allan Group was declared open for business in early 1992.

I would get into serious trouble – no, I am always in that – more serious trouble if I did not mention somewhere in this book the impact of the immediate family on the business. I have already recorded Mollie's input in

*Above:*
**The Allan family celebrating 50 years of transport publishing on the Dart Valley Railway at Kingswear. Left to right: Ian, Mollie, Gillian, David, Jane and Paul.**

the early days but as deputy chairman of the Group Company and a very active director in the Hotel Company, she has played a great part in the operation and development of the Company, even to the extent of pouring the healing balm of consolation all over me when everything has gone wrong. She has listened patiently to my tale of woe or conversely working me up to fever pitch to deal with some matter which she has been concerned about and which I appeared to have overlooked.

David and Paul, having taken over the management of their respective subsidiary companies, gradually worked their way into the central administration, commonly known as 'Group' and their input steadily changed the outlook from that of the 1950s and 1960s to the 1990s and beyond. Thus the family three, together with respective wives plus our two accountant colleagues, Norman Miles, now partly retired, and his successor Howard Somerville, form the Group board which determines overall policy. The next generation now beginning to snap at our heels led by nine-year-old Marc, who shows signs of becoming a railway enthusiast, and ever ready to come for a train ride or get involved with the Cockcrow Railway, followed by Nicholas, Ben, Victoria, Kate and Sam, none of whom seems to have been impregnated by the bug but nevertheless do allow themselves to be taken for a ride on some occasions if duly bribed.

We have tried to maintain contacts with all those who have been involved with the Company over the years and we hold an annual geriatric get-together at Broadway. There seem to be more and more each year and not only from 'IA' Companies. Links are still very much alive with the chaps we have 'taken over' including John Parke, John Tallack and Bill Cornwell from *Modern Transport* days, all of whom are very much alive and kicking.

We are a 'family business' and we like to think that the feeling goes beyond the strict confines of the family. To this end we try to bring all the directors and senior managers together at least twice a year and the culmination of such meetings is the solo presented by Derick Sharp, the Managing Director of our printing company who, for the last 20 years, has sung his 'winkle' song on all occasions except when his wife is present when we discovered who really wears the trousers in his household.

When I referred earlier rather lightly to the refurbishment of our printing company, I was understating it a bit. We invested £1,000,000 in new equipment – fast-running five-colour 'perfecter' printing machines and the very latest in typesetting, platemaking and photographic equipment and it was Derick Sharp who masterminded the whole thing. In full consultation with his dog Harvey with whom he discussed the plan every night between 11 and 12 during the course of their evening stroll and his two colleagues, Jon Bingham and Nick Lerwill, with whom he did not stroll, he directed builders, plumbers, partition fitters, double glaziers and finished up with a very high powered and modern factory.

It is impossible to mention the myriad people who have served the company over the years but we have always valued the contributions made by an elite band of ladies, several of whom have been with us for over 20 years, some even longer. The doyen of them all was Hilda Harmer who put in 27 years; Margaret Knight, who secretaried for Willie Brett and Charles Hemmings and latterly me, also gave us the best 27 years of her life; Betty Reeve, who still carries on after 23 years, has looked after editorial directors from 1969 until she took me and David over from Margaret Knight in the Group office; Mary Beckerson, another 25-year badge holder, masterminded the sales office of Ian Allan Ltd before transferring in 1991 to Chase Organics. And there was Anne White (née Grover) who not only did a splendid secretarying job but also managed the Company football team and played (not very well) in the ladies' team until she laddered her tights. The total length of service of these ladies and our rep force which whom they all worked, must tot up to well over 200 years.

And so we have hit the 50th Anniversary of the publication of that first *abc of Southern Locomotives* in 1942 amidst the storming sessions of Hitler, Grasemann and Bulleid, through the bombs and doodlebugs of Waterloo to the squalor of Vauxhall Bridge Road and the deer and sewage of Hampton Court to the green fields of Shepperton and the rapid approach of my personal 70th milestone. I have enjoyed most of it, especially my wife, children, children-in-law and grandchildren not to mention my parents and grandparents, mother-in-law, friends and staff, to all of whom I am eternally grateful. I didn't much care for having a leg sawn off at the age of 15 or spending seven days in hospital at 65. I did not enjoy being nearly broke in 1950 but I have enjoyed almost every other minute of a life in which work and play have mingled without definition, and strongly recommend everyone to try to ensure that they engage themselves in a job which is at once a breadwinner and a hobby and when they never quite know which is which, and to have plenty of outside interests too.